Energy Healing for Mental Health

EXPLORING DIS-EASE
THROUGH THE LENS OF THE
ENERGETIC BODY

Adrian Campbell, PhD

Illustrations by
Tricia Dietrich & Shawn Palmer

Copyright ©2024 by Adrian Campbell, PhD
Cover and internal design by Adrian Campbell, PhD

All rights reserved. No part of this book may be reproduced in any form or by any electronic or mechanical means including information storage and retrieval systems - except in the case of brief quotations embodied in critical articles or reviews - without permission in writing from Adrian Campbell, PhD.

Published by Adrian Campbell, PhD
www.EnergeticPsyche.com

Table of Contents

Chapter 1: Understanding our Dis-Ease 6

   Understanding Dis-Ease 8

      Symptoms of Dis-ease 10

      Dis-ease and the Body 11

      Empowerment through Self Agency 12

   The Energetic Self 19

      The Aura 20

      The Chakra System 20

Chapter 2: Understanding Reiki Energy Healing 24

   What is Energy Healing? 25

   Reiki Energy Healing 26

      Reiki Masters & Attunements 27

Chapter 3: Energy Healing Techniques 32

   Energy Healing & its Uses 33

   Working with Reiki 34

      Getting the Flow Going 36

      FAQs About Working with Reiki 37

   Reiki Self-Sessions 42

      Intuitive Self-Session 42

      Standard Self-Session Hand Placements 44

      Alternative Sessions and Hand Placements 48

      Guided Intuitive Self-Session Meditation 49

Chapter 4: Energy Healing for Specific Purposes 56

Using Reiki Symbols 58

- The Power Symbol 59
- The Mental & Emotional Healing Symbol 60
- The Distance Healing Symbol 60

Additional Uses for Reiki 63

Chapter 5: The Healing Power of Crystals 66

The Healing Power of Crystals 68

Using Reiki with Crystals 69

Creating Crystal "Healing Bundles" 70

Creating Crystal Grids 74

Chapter 6: Exploring Dis-ease through the Energetic Body 78

Exploring Dis-ease through the Energetic Body 79

Types of Imbalances in the Chakra System 81

Healing Dis-ease through the Chakra System 82

Understanding Energetic Contributions 83

Chapter 7: Exploring Your Chakra System 88

Base Chakra 89

Sacral Chakra 95

Solar Plexus Chakra 103

Heart Chakra 111

Throat Chakra 118

Brow Chakra 125

Crown Chakra 131

Chapter 8: Co-Creating Your Future through Daily Practice 140

Co-Creation and Manifestation 142

Creating a Daily Practice 147

Appendix: Meditations 160

Body Scan Meditation 162

Yoga Nidra 165

Lovingkindness – Metta Meditation 172

Chapter 1

Understanding Our Dis-Ease

"The concept of total wellness recognizes that our every thought, word, and behavior affects our greater health and well-being. And we, in turn, are affected not only emotionally but also physically and spiritually."

~ Greg Anderson ~

Understanding Dis-Ease

Life isn't meant to be all sunshine and rainbows, however, creating a life of ease and contentment, one with balance between the highs and the lows is something you can work towards, and something you deserve.

Dis-ease is essentially the opposite of *ease*, it is the lack of ease or comfort. It is one half to a whole, and if we are to live in balance it is important to realize that there will always be moments of dis-ease, that is the way it is, the way it is meant to be. And that is actually a good thing!

Now, hear me out… dis-ease, or lack of comfort often occurs during some of our most challenging moments in life, and it is exactly those challenges that help us to become the beautiful, strong, resilient beings we are. If everything was easy, if you never met a challenge, I guarantee you wouldn't be half of who you are. And you are amazing (even if you don't believe it yet).

Now I know this is a book about energy healing for mental health, so there may be a few of you reading this and thinking "Yea Adrian, challenges are great and all, but if I could have skipped all that I wouldn't have all these jacked up trauma responses!" I hear you, BUT again hear me out, trauma responses aren't actually all bad, if you can bring awareness to them and use them in a way that serves you, versus being controlled by them.

So much of our long-term or chronic dis-ease comes from a lack of awareness. As we go through these challenging moments in our lives and develop patterns of behavior, some of which can be called trauma responses, they tend to take up residence in the unconscious mind. Unfortunately when they live down there, we lack an awareness of how they are controlling us and impacting our lives. A good friend and colleague of mine, Dr. Mindy Nettifee, explains it as something like wind or electricity… you can't see it but you can observe the impact of it.

In the case of unconscious trauma responses and learned behavioral patterns, we can see them play out in our lives through consistent and repeated difficulties in our relationships, trouble finding a job that fulfills us, repeated unhealthy choices, and more. After doing something you later regret, maybe an outburst at work, a comment to a friend that was unkind, or even a purchase you couldn't afford… you may ask yourself "What was I thinking?!", and well, the cause most likely stems from energies at work in the unconscious mind.

Sound familiar? You aren't alone. So how do we fix this? How do you take control of your life? Well, first step is realizing you will ever only have so much control. Working with the unconscious mind is all about being in relationship with those parts of you that live there. To really work on your symptoms of dis-ease, to get to the root cause of things, it has to be a team effort.

Throughout this book I will share several different methods of coming into relationship with your unconscious, through the energetic body. As with any relationship there will be a give and take, a share and receive component. To truly move into relationship you must be willing to listen and give respect, and this is no different. And, it will take time, how much mostly depends on how attached you are to the beliefs and patterns of behavior that support the dis-ease.

Now that might sound crazy, I know. But believe it or not, you are an amazingly powerful being with the ability to create and change your own reality. However, when we are unconscious to what is driving our lives, we often just end up along for the ride. As you bring more and more of your shadow elements into the light you will have to opportunity to decide what to keep and what to release, what energies to shift, and what to integrate more fully. You have the power to do all of this and more, right now, in this moment. You just might not be able to *see*, so we're gonna work on that.

Symptoms of Dis-ease

I wanted to take a few moments to talk about the difference between symptoms of dis-ease and actual disorders. In this world of ours it seems like EVERYTHING has become a disorder and too many of us just accept these labels that are placed on us as if they were part of our identity. The medical industry seems to have a pill for *everything* and the American culture pushes us to just drug the symptoms away so we can get back to work, back to *life*. But is it the life you are meant to be living? If you are experiencing symptoms of dis-ease, something is WRONG. Symptoms are a cry for help and when we drug them into silence we don't solve the problem, we just delay the inevitable. Eventually the drugs won't be strong enough and new symptoms will break through and start wreaking havoc.

Now, please hear me when I say I do not expect you to quit your job and run off to a life of ease in the Caribbean because you have an anxiety attack at work. Let's be realistic, I know that sometimes there isn't much you can do to change the situation you are in or the people that surround you, at least not right away. What I am asking you to consider is listening to your symptoms, exploring them, maybe following where they lead, and just put a little effort into figuring out what they might be trying to tell you.

I am also asking you to take responsibility for your well-being and not give all power over your health to an outside authority. Please use your resources, talk to your doctors, therapists, etc., but remember at the end of the day YOU are the ultimate authority in your life. YOU know what is best for you and any relationship with an outside authority should be a partnership between both of you.

Dis-ease and the Body

When working to address dis-ease, western culture has historically focused on the physical body, viewing our all of our dis-ease as being related to physical dysfunction of some kind. In fact, into the early 1900s it was still believed by many that emotional or mental dis-ease in women, was caused by things such as a tendency for fluids to get held in the uterus, or because the uterus *apparently* had a habit of wandering about the female body.

In the late 1800s and early 1900s the field of psychology came into being through the work of pioneers like Sigmund Freud and Carl Jung. This is when we began to realize that our entire existence in not wholly explainable by the status of the physical body. The mental/emotional body began to get more attention and has since come to be recognized as not only a significant contributor to our general sense of ease or dis-ease, but also our physical health. This was partly brought forward by a new field, founded by the work of Wilheim Reich called Somatic Psychology. Though his work began in the early 20th century, it wasn't until decades later, and only recently, that it has become a more widely accepted field, encouraged through the work of people like Peter Levine, Bessel Van Der Kolk, Stephen Porges, and more.

Today a more holistic approach, one that includes the physical and mental/emotional body as contributors to our overall well-being, has become more common. However, a heavy focus is still placed upon the physical, with many practitioners choosing to address even mental and emotional dis-ease as a dysfunction of the brain, central nervous system, or other body part. What is NOT being addressed by most wellness practitioners is the internal energetic and psychic world of the individual.

Now, when I say psychic, I am not talking about having special mind reading powers. Use of the word psychic in this book, and in Jungian (those who study the work of Carl Jung) psychology, stems from the Latin word "Psyche", meaning the soul, mind, or spirit, which inhabits the physical body. So "Physic" is that having to do with the soul, mind, or spirit, within an individual. And technically, the term "Psychology" is the study (-ology) of Psyche. But again, if we look at the evolution of the field of psychology, we will see that though it started with Freud and Jung and did in fact focus on the inner psychic world of the individual, over time it has shifted away from the soul to focus once again on the body as a primary source of dis-ease.

I am not telling you that dis-ease doesn't come from the physical body, because it definitely can; anyone that suffers with chronic pain can attest to that. What I am trying to explain is that it isn't the *only* place our dis-ease stems from, and as you move through this book I hope you will see that not only does the individual psyche contribute significantly to our state of ease or dis-ease, it has the power to change it.

Empowerment through Self Agency

Too often we seek out wellness professionals wanting to be *fixed,* believing that we are broken if we don't fit some culturally acceptable mold. We have been conditioned, both consciously and unconsciously, to believe that the power to heal lies outside of ourselves. It is of the upmost importance that you try to shift your thinking, that you try to understand that you have been carefully and intentionally created, and that deep down YOU are the one that knows what is best for you. For true healing to take place it is imperative that you engage in the process.

As individuals we have the ultimate power in deciding whether we will get well. If you are not onboard, there isn't much a professional can do for you.

We all make direct contributions to the state we are in. These show up as past actions, current behaviors and beliefs, and future desires. When we ignore or refuse to own our past, when we don't take responsibility for our current behaviors, when we don't create goals and set intentions, we are allowing our ship to run adrift in the ocean of life.

In order to heal, to create a life of comfort and ease, we must take responsibility for our own healing. It is through this responsibility that we empower ourselves to heal.

Everything Is Energy Meditation

(Feel free to record yourself reciting this meditation and then listen to it as many times as you'd like.)

Begin by sitting or lying down. I invite you to close your eyes or lower your gaze.

Allow your body to flex or stretch in any way that it needs. Maybe roll your head from side to side, perhaps forward and backward…Wiggle and stretch your fingers or toes... Roll your wrists in circles, maybe your shoulders, forwards and then backwards... Take a few moments to allow any physical energy to find release through subtle movement… when you are ready, settle into a position that you will find comfortable for the duration of the meditation.

Now I'll invite you to take a few deep breaths. Breathing in, nice and deep, expanding the lungs, the belly… and then exhaling out every last bit of air from your lungs. Breath in again, nice deep breath, again expanding the lungs, the belly, really filling yourself all the way up, and then exhaling out every last bit of air, feeling your navel draw in towards the spine, until you breathe in again, one last deep breath, expanding, filling, and then one final exhale through the mouth, letting it all go

Now release any control of the breath and return to your natural breathing.

Imagine within you, there is a spark. This is the spark that lives within us all, that fuels us, that keeps us up and moving, this is the spark of life. Find this spark within you, deep within your being, within your heart, and allow all of your attention to focus on this spark... notice that this spark is not stagnant, but alive. Watch it as it glows, pulses, shifts in size and strength… notice that the glow from this spark does not end at the edges of it's source, but rather, the glow extends… follow the glow of this spark, the warm golden glow of this spark as it extends out throughout your body… feeling the glow move out from the chest, warming you as it goes... across the abdomen... down through the hips and the legs... grounding you to the earth... flowing up into the neck and shoulders... down the arms, and into the fingers... up and along the jaw, over the cheeks, ears, eyes, and forehead... finding it's way to the crown of your head and stretching up and outward, connecting you to all that is above and beyond... be with this feeling for a few moments, allowing the warmth of this glow to wash over your entire being, feeling yourself safely grounded to the earth beneath you and connected to all that is above.

Remembering to breathe... allowing this golden glow to completely envelop you... feeling yourself in your body, your body enveloped by this beautiful glow... keeping your eyes closed, allow yourself to once again move any part of your body that would like to move, gently flexing, rolling, stretching, all while feeling yourself emanating with this beautiful golden glow. Allow yourself to inwardly watch the energy shift as you begin to move your body. How does it flex along with you? How does it shift and change in tandem with your movement? Spend some time in this space, being in movement with the energy of the spark.

When you are ready I invite you to slowly and gently crack open your eyelids, but only a bit... allow yourself to imagine you see this glow surrounding every inch of your body. Extending out from your skin into the world around you... what does it look like? How does it feel? Does it shift as you wiggle your fingers? Move your arms? Spend a few moments here in this space.

Now I invite you to slowly open your eyes fully and take a few moments to reflect on your experience in your journal.

Take a few moments and reflect on your experience during the meditation...

I encourage journaling after any meditation or energy healing session, as it helps anchor any healing energies here in the physical plane and can act as a reminder of things that may have come forward from beyond the conscious mind.

Remember that reflections can be anything you feel, and don't have to make sense to anyone, not even you. Written journal entries, images, or even just colors and shapes can all be helpful as we try to capture our experiences. Sometimes it is the simple lines that lead us to the greater discoveries down the road. It is up to you, use the space in your journal as you choose.

_____
_____
_____
_____
_____
_____
_____
_____

The Energetic Self

We are energy, the animals and plants around us are energy. Even the inanimate objects that we observe, touch, and use on a daily basis are energy. We are all made up of atoms, held together by varying frequencies which determine what shape and form we will take.

And just like the spark of energy within you that you experienced during the meditation, these energies are not stagnant, they are not isolated, they are not alone. We are all connected to one another, influence one another, and shape the daily reality that we get to experience. These energies are a representation, or manifestation of our entire self, they are a combination of the energetic psyche and the energetic body. Just as the individual psyche will shape the experience for the body it resides within, collectively our joined psyches shape the world we all live in. The power that we hold to shape our experience is incredible! The power YOU hold to shape your world and the world of those around you into something beautiful is unfathomable. You are more powerful than you might ever believe.

The energetic self is an energetic representation of our mind, body, and spirit, containing ripples, scars, and spots, just as our physical body does. It is made up of the psyche, aura and chakra system, and supported by what is known as life force energy.

Life force energy, known across the world by different names, such as Chi, Ki, or Prana is what makes living beings different than the inanimate objects around us. Life force energy is a vital energy, which when low or restricted makes one more vulnerable to illness or injury. It is through intention and the practices that support it, that life force energy can be directed in a way that allows us to ensure it flows freely throughout our being encouraging over all wellness.

The Aura

As you experienced in the meditation, our life force energy is not contained by our physical body. Our energy extends out beyond our skin and into the world around us, and is often called the aura or bioenergetic field. The size, shape and color can differ from hour to hour, or day to day, depending on how we feel based off experiences both past and present. Though, it is widely believed that we each have an underlying color with us from birth, that represents our foundational traits.

What I have found in my studies and practice is that when we feel safe and loved, when we are happy and excited, our auras tend to be big and bright, extending up to 10ft or more from our bodies. However, when one is sick, injured, or sad and perhaps not wanting to engage with the world, the aura is pulled in close to the body, extending maybe half an inch, if at all. Remember the aura is an extension of the self and reacts to our experiences like the physical body might.

The aura is the energetic manifestation of your thoughts, feelings, and beliefs, both conscious and unconscious. It is affected by what you experience, just as much as the mind and central nervous system. It is often how we first interact with the world around us, how we pick up and give off *vibes*. It is our auras that allow us to *feel* the energy in a room based on the energetic connections we share. Unfortunately, because we typically aren't aware of our auras, we don't pay them enough attention.

The Chakra System

The chakra system is the metaphorical bridge between consciousness and matter. It is a part of our energetic body, and it affects our physical being (breathing, heart rate, and metabolism) just as emotions do.

The status of our chakra system directly affects the way we receive and interpret information, changing how we interact with the world.

Becoming more familiar with your system, the way you move and hold energy, will help you improve the health of your chakra system and your life overall.

There are seven major chakras, each of which represents a specific type of energy.

1	Root/Base	Red	Survival/Grounding/Prosperity
2	Sacral	Orange	Emotions/Sexuality/Family/Feminine
3	Solar Plexus	Yellow	Power/Autonomy/Will/Masculine
4	Heart	Green	Compassion/Self Love
5	Throat	Light Blue	Self-Expression/Communication
6	Brow/Third Eye	Indigo	Intuition/ Creativity
7	Crown	Purple	Consciousness/Spirit

Too often the chakras are viewed as discrete components which can be worked with individually, but this cannot be further from the truth. All the chakras work together in a holistic manner to maintain balance throughout your energetic system. When one chakra is out of balance, the entire system is affected.

The lower half of the system (chakras 1-3) focus on the physical realties of our existence, and the upper half of the system (chakras 5-7) focus on more ethereal and imaginative states. Chakra 4 connects the upper and lower halves of the system, putting love and compassion at the center of all things.

It is important that neither the upper nor lower half of the system is given preference, but rather, one should strive to bring the entire system into balance.

Crown

Brow

Throat

Heart

Solar Plexus

Sacral

Base/Root

Color in each chakra with the associated color listed in the chart

Chapter 2

Understanding Reiki Energy Healing

What is Energy Healing?

As mentioned in the previous section, we all have a special life force energy that flows within us. This energy known as Chi, Ki, or Prana, flows through us like a river, ensuring that our energy doesn't become stagnant, or still.

Unfortunately, life isn't always easy, and it's a given that we will experience different injuries, either physical, mental, or emotional, throughout our lifetimes. These injuries create what are known as energetic blocks, the boulders in the river of life force energy.

Energetic blocks negatively impact our well-being by restricting the flow of our life force energy. These energetic blocks can manifest as symptoms of disease, in the physical, mental/emotional, and energetic body. Depending on the severity of the injury, and the length of time we endure its affects, our life force energy may be reduced to a trickle, or in some cases, these energetic blocks can be large enough to completely stop the flow.

When the flow of our life force energy is interrupted, the way we interact with the world changes, it becomes distorted as our system tries to adjust to the interference. Over time if the blocks are not healed, we create new patterns of functioning, psychologically, emotionally, and physically, which only act to reinforce the block and continue to limit flow.

Think about the impact of a broken ankle… physically the bone is broken with symptoms of swelling, inability to use that area of the body, an adjustment in how the entire body will be able to move for a period of time, and of course, physical pain. Mentally and emotionally the injury may create feelings of frustration, anger, sadness, and more, depending on how the injury occurred and how long it will take to heal. Energetically, a severe broken ankle can create a blockage in the flow of life force energy, restricting flow to the foot, which if not acknowledged can lead to lasting issues in that area of the body, even once the ankle has physically healed.

Energy healing works through focused intention to remove these blocks, so that our life force energy can flow freely again, allowing us to heal. In the case of the broken ankle, energy healing can assist in maintaining a healthy flow of energy to the foot while the ankle heals, as well as encourage healing to occur in the area of the broken bone.

Anyone can access energy healing, to help themselves or others, as we are all made up of energy and have the power of intention available to us. However, depending on your current energetic state, working with your own energy may cause more harm than good, and over time using your own energy to heal can be exhausting.

To avoid wearing yourself out by using your own energy, there are several other forms of energy healing available which allow you to work with source energy, rather than your own. Through use of some of these other types, such as Reiki, you have the ability to help yourself and others without becoming depleted.

Reiki Energy Healing

Reiki energy is a specific form of energy, considered to be a direct connection to the source of life force energy. Out of the different types of energy healing available, the International Center of Reiki Training (ICRT) believes Reiki to be of the highest frequency and to be guided by spiritual consciousness.

Reiki originated in Japan, discovered by Usui Sensei on Mt. Kumara in 1922. Usui Sensei had several clinics and trained over 2,000 students, receiving an award from the Japanese government for the healing work he did after the devastating earthquake in 1923. Reiki was brought to the west by Mrs. Takata in 1937 but did not gain in popularity until the 1970s due in part to the stigma attached to anything considered Japanese after World War II.

When working with Reiki energy you are connected to the source of life force energy, a spiritually guided energy which when invited, will remove any blocks that may be present in yourself or others. Reiki Practitioners do not heal, but rather act as a channel for the Reiki energy, allowing it to flow through them to another. Because of this, the Reiki Practitioner's own energies will never be depleted, but rather, they will be continually refreshed as the Practitioner receives a session every time they give one.

As Reiki is guided by spiritual consciousness it will never do any harm and will never go against anyone's will. Reiki energy will always act in a way that is in the best interest of the person receiving the Reiki energy.

Reiki Masters & Attunements

People often wonder why an attunement is necessary. Because if we all have access to life force energy, why can't we just kick it up a notch? Reach out directly? Why do we need a "Master"? Is Reiki a cult?!?! No, Reiki is not a cult. I promise.

And being a Reiki Master does not give you any authority over anyone else, it merely means that you have completed the required training and associated attunements, and that you can teach others to do the same.

Though we do all have access to life force energy, we only have access to it at a specific frequency. The frequency of Reiki energy is higher than our normal frequency, and each new level of Reiki connects the Practitioner to a higher level of energy.

The Reiki Master who is attuned to the higher frequencies channel them during the attunements, helping new Practitioners connect. The attunement process is like an introduction made by the Reiki Master, between the new Practitioner and the new frequency of Reiki Energy.

During the attunement process the new frequency of energy, led by spiritual consciousness, enters the student and makes necessary accommodations or adjustments in the new Practitioner's energetic body and consciousness, to allow the Practitioner the ability to channel Reiki energy. Some students report mystical experiences such as personal messages from guides and loved ones, visions, increased psychic abilities, past life experiences, and enhanced intuitive awareness. Others report merely the feeling of a gentle warm glow enveloping their body.

In a new Reiki Practitioner, there are often energetic blocks, unhealthy beliefs, or patterns of behavior that need to be released through a cleansing process. The cleansing process begins during the attunement and typically lasts 21 days (3 days for each of the 7 major chakras). This process may cause physical symptoms such as a headache, stomachache, or tiredness as toxins are cleared from the body. You may also experience temporary emotional or behavioral changes, such as increased joy or sadness, unexplained moodiness, changes in your energy levels, or interesting dreams, as the unhealthy beliefs and negative patterns are released. What is most important during this time is to be aware of your symptoms and give yourself the care you need, whether it is more rest and fluids, perhaps a shift to your schedule, dietary changes, or spending more time in quiet contemplation around your current way of life and any long-term changes that may need to take place. If at any time you feel the need to seek medical attention it is important that you do so.

Every attunement and cleansing experience is unique to the individual, fine-tuned by the spiritually guided energy to meet the needs of each new Reiki Practitioner. No experience is better than another, as each is uniquely crafted for the individual. Be careful not to let your expectations lead you astray. Trust that what is, is exactly what it should be.

The symbol for Reiki is in Japanese Kanji and depicts the heavens above, the earth below, and the human healer as the in between.

Clouds/Heaven

Human Healer
(Mind - Body - Spirit)

Earth

Life Force Energy

Chapter 3

Energy Healing Techniques

Energy Healing & its Uses

As a direct connection to source energy, there isn't much that Reiki can't be used for. Any time you would send an intention, thought, prayer, or blessing, you can send Reiki with it. Sure, you can use Reiki as part of an in-depth meditative practice or personal session, but it can also be used while you do something as simple as watering your plants.

Reiki can be used to clear energetic blockages in anyone or any "thing" that has life force energy flowing through it. That means YOU, your significant other, your kids, friends and family, pets and wild animals, your food, houseplants, forests, jungles, rivers, oceans, the WORLD! There really is no limit to what you can do with Reiki.

Reiki can also be used to clear and seal the energy in spaces you live and work in to create a healthier energetic balance in your environment. And you can even use Reiki to affect the energy in past, present, and future situations.

To create the basic foundation for your Reiki practice, you can simply start with one of the two versions of the self-sessions described in this book, maybe add in a little Reiki to charge some crystals to help create healthier habits and support intention setting. But know this is just the beginning…

Reiki is a very personal experience, and you will find your own unique way to work with this energy. I encourage you to practice what I share with you here, and then let it naturally adapt and progress on its own. After a while, you will find what works best for you and develop your own practice based on your unique energetic needs.

Working with Reiki

The techniques for working with Reiki are simple and require no special skills, anyone can work with Reiki! All it takes is an attunement and you will be able to access Reiki energy for the rest of your life.

To get Reiki to flow, all you have to do is ask it to do so. In the beginning it may help to have a code word or starting phrase like "Reiki Go!". I invite you to get creative and see what feels right.

While it is not necessary to be in a meditative state to practice Reiki, taking a few moments to focus and center yourself is suggested. You may begin by placing your hands in prayer position, in front of your body (also known as Gassho meditation). Take a few deep breaths and ask for guidance in setting your ego aside. As mentioned previously, you are a vessel for Reiki to flow through, and as such, it is important that you don't interfere by getting in the way. Source energy knows what is best, and if you let your ego take over you won't give source energy the space it needs to do the work that it knows needs to be done.

At this point you may also want to invite spirit guides, ancestors, or other healing entities to join you. I typically just call their name and ask that they support the healing that needs to take place. Remembering once again, that I am not in charge, but rather being given an opportunity to share and receive healing by practicing Reiki. For example I may say something like "Dear Archangel Michael, please hear me as I ask for your help in this Reiki healing session" or "Dear beings of the highest heavens, dear Jesus, dear Quan Yin, I invite you to join me in this Reiki healing session. Dear spirit guides, ancestors, and ascended masters of the highest frequencies, I invite you to join me in this Reiki healing session."

Now if you don't currently have any guides you work with, that is ok. It is up to you whether or not you would like to work with guides. Over time they may come to you as you develop your energy healing practice, or you may decide to seek them out. Either way, it will not change your ability to practice Reiki, it's just an additional element you may want to add to your practice.

Next, set the intention for your practice by mentally stating what it is you are asking to be healed. For example, you can say things like "I ask that this session provide me with the healing that is in my best interest", or "Please send my plants healing energy to help them grow healthy and strong", or "Please provide me with the healing that I need so that I can sleep well tonight". The wording doesn't have to be specific, so don't fuss over terminology. Just be sure to take the time and set your intention in whatever way feels best for you.

Next you will want to imagine your crown chakra opening up as wide as it can go and asking Reiki to begin flowing, "Reiki Go!". In your mind's eye, see the brilliant white light of Reiki energy flowing down from the heavens into your crown chakra, and flowing out through your heart and hands in a continuous stream of warm and loving energy.

Getting the Flow Going

1. Begin by placing your hands in prayer position (Gassho meditation).

2. Take a few deeps breaths.

3. Ask for guidance in setting your ego aside.

4. Invite any guides you would like to participate in the session.

5. Set your intentions.

6. Imagine your crown chakra opening up wide and ask for Reiki to flow.

7. With your mind's eye, see the brilliant white light of Reiki energy flowing into your crown chakra.

8. Concentrate of the continuous flow of Reiki into the crown chakra and down into the heart and hands.

© 2024, Adrian Campbell, PhD

FAQs About Working with Reiki

Q: What should it feel like?

It is different for everyone, but most people feel warmth in their palms, and some feel tingling. When you use Reiki on someone else an energetic resonance is created between your two energies and the warmth or tingling will feel different as you move across different areas of their body.

The sensation usually increases when energy flow is good, and decreases when flow is low or blocked, but that may not always be true. In the case of an excessive chakra, there will be more warmth/tingling and the sensation should decrease as you flow Reiki into the chakra.

Q: What if I don't feel anything?

That is perfectly OK. Remember that everyone's relationship with Reiki is unique and just because you don't feel it, doesn't mean it isn't working. Over time, as you work with Reiki more often and for longer periods of time you may begin to feel sensations in your hands, or you may not. You may feel an increased sense of intuition, you may not. Unfortunately, I am not in charge and can't tell you exactly what spirit has in mind for you.

One thing I can tell you for sure, is that for the few students I have had that didn't feel anything, the people they practiced on sure did! Out of the 100+ students I have had come through my classes I have never had someone lacking sensation in their hands give an unsuccessful session. I invite you to trust that you are exactly where you are supposed to be, and that whatever you experience is exactly as it should.

Q: Can I do Reiki anywhere?

Absolutely! However, the experience will be different as your environment changes. For example, you can give yourself Reiki in a quiet room, with low light, while relaxing music plays, and you lay quietly relaxing on couch or in bed, or you can give yourself Reiki while sitting at your desk at work. In both cases you will receive exactly what you need from Reiki energy, as long as you can focus enough to maintain the flow of Reiki.

When giving Reiki to animals, plants, environments, and communities I would recommend finding a quiet place where you can concentrate on your healing intentions. But that doesn't mean that if you are out on a lake you can't ask for Reiki to flow and send some Reiki love into the waters around you, or if you are out on a walk maybe you take a moment to place your hands on a tree and share Reiki through a gentle touch. Use your imagination and be creative. See what feels good, what works, what doesn't, and then adjust your practice accordingly.

Q: How long should I do it for?

Depends on the situation. A self-session can be as long or as short as you'd like. Maybe you give yourself just a few minutes of Reiki before walking into an important meeting, or maybe you give yourself a 30min session every morning and evening. When it comes to self-session, I would say just go with what feels right, and at the end of the day if you aren't sure just follow the standard hand placements, staying in each one for a couple minutes.

Remember that when using Reiki energy you will never become depleted, as you receive a session every time you give one, but your physical body may become tired. Be mindful of how you hold your arms, bend your body, etc., and don't be afraid to use a pillow, chair or the wall to support yourself during a session.

Q: Can I spread my fingers, or do they have to stay together?

It is recommended that you keep your fingers together as a way to "cup" the energy coming out of the palm chakras but go ahead and try both and see how each feel. For me the energy feels dispersed, lessened, when I spread my fingers, so I like to keep them together, like in the image below. But maybe for you it will be different. Again, this is a unique experience for every individual, so play around with it and do what feels right.

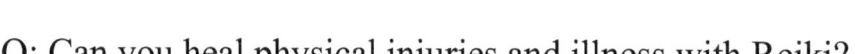

Q: Can you heal physical injuries and illness with Reiki?

Reiki energy can be helpful towards healing physical injuries and illnesses; however, it should never take the place of professional medical care for humans or animals. Reiki, like many other holistic practices, should be treated as complementary care, to be used in tandem with professional medical practices.

Q: How many sessions does it take to clear an energetic block?

Honestly, there is no way to know for sure. Don't pressure yourself, give it grace, and remember we don't always have the widest view of the world, not compared to Spirit. Depending on how old the block is, or why it is there, it may take some time. If you've developed behavior or thought patterns that reinforce it, you will need to do work in that area as well before the block can be cleared. And well, some blocks are just going to end up a part of our energetic make-up, and that is ok too. When doing this work, we need to trust that Spirit, or Universal Consciousness, knows what is best for us and just trust. Do what you can to heal and trust that all will be as it should. And if you are ever struggling, don't hesitate to reach out for professional help.

Q: Will I pick up negative energy when I work with Reiki?

When doing sessions on yourself you shouldn't have to worry too much about this. But, if you are working on clearing an environment or space that is icky, or working to heal traumatic situations from the past, you might what to clean your energy when you are done.

To cleanse your aura you will swipe your hands, still charged with Reiki, across your body diagonally in each direction, and down each arm (see the images on following page). This is traditionally called Kenyoku or Dry Bathing. You may also want to physically wash your hands with soap and water.

Kenyoku aka Dry Bathing

Reiki Self-Sessions

In this section I will share two different ways of giving yourself a Reiki session, the intuitive method and using standard hand placements. As I mentioned above, these methods are merely a foundation, and if you are guided to practice in a way that is different than either of these methods, please feel free to do so.

Self-sessions are a wonderful way to incorporate self-care in your daily routine. By practicing Reiki daily, you are able to reap the preventative benefits of Reiki as well as the reactive, such as a stronger immune system, enhanced intuition, a calmer central nervous system, increased energy, improved concentration, better sleep, and more.

I recommend a self-session twice a day, once in the morning and again when you get home or before bed. Self-sessions can get you ready for the day ahead, by wrapping you in a sort of energetic armor, allowing anything not meant for you to bounce right off. It can also act as an energetic detox at the end of the day, helping you clean away anything you may have energetically picked up or experienced throughout your daily interactions and activities.

Intuitive Self-Session

This is my typical go-to for self-sessions. Though I often incorporate a lot of the standard positions in my intuitive session, I usually just do them in the order that feels right to me. Feel free to be flexible and go with whatever you are guided to do.

I begin my intuitive sessions as I would any session, hands in prayer position, asking to set my ego aside, inviting my guides to assist in my healing, and asking Reiki to flow. I then raise my hands to my third eye and ask for guidance so that I may support Reiki in sending me the healing that is in my best interest.

I then move my hands to wherever I feel guided to do so and leave them in that position until I feel guided to change.

Standard Self-Session Hand Placements

The standard hand placements are a great place to start when giving yourself Reiki. They are also a great place to fall back to if you've had a hard day, you're tired, or your intuition just isn't cooperating.

You can follow along with the images on the following pages, giving each position between 1-3 minutes, longer if you'd like.

Hand placements for the head help us treat the Crown and Brow chakras. Individuals often report seeing swirling purple colors when working in this area and find these placements to be extremely helpful when they are feeling isolated, overly grounded, or intuitively stuck.

© 2024, Adrian Campbell, PhD

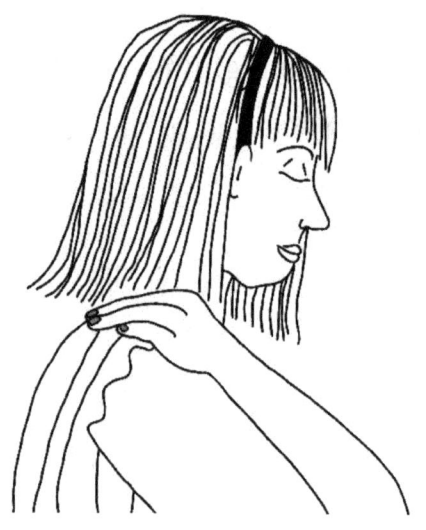

Hand placements at the neck and shoulders work with the energies of the Throat chakra.

There is often a lot of stress carried upon the shoulders, silently burdened, ignored and pushed aside.

The top hand placement works to help loosen the stress, to break up the mass into more manageable bits to be cleared away.

The bottom hand placement brings in the heart chakra and helps us remember we don't have to suffer in silence, and we are never alone.

This hand placement reminds us to love ourselves, to give ourselves a break. By working with the Heart chakra, we encourage self-compassion, remembering we're doing the best we can.

Heavy energies and emotions can often be found in the abdomen and groin areas, as they often house what we energetically avoid and push away.

In this space is the Solar Plexus, the Sacral, and the Root chakras. The hub of self-esteem, self-worth, sensuality, family, and safety.

Be gentle with yourself in this space. Try not to rush any work you do here, but rather be patient with what comes forward. And perhaps practice allowing that which is uncomfortable to surface and be set free.

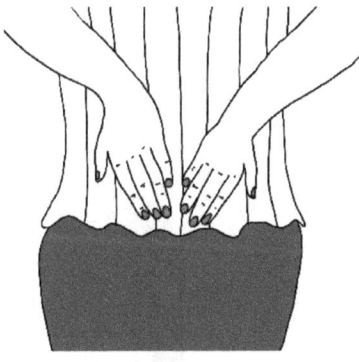

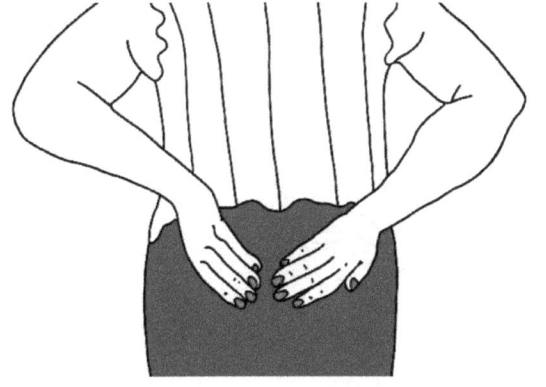

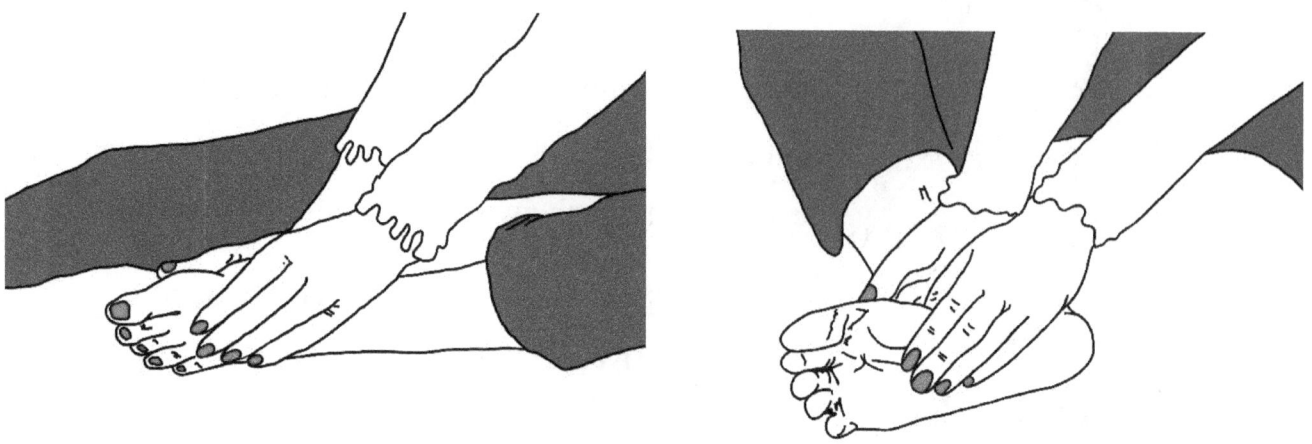

The feet are our primary source of grounding, and unfortunately moves through untold quantities of energetic junk each and every day.

They are one of the most important parts of body, and yet they are often the most overworked and under cared for.

Give the feet the time they deserve so they may continue to allow a strong connection to the grounding energies of Earth, which help to keep you safe, healthy, and strong.

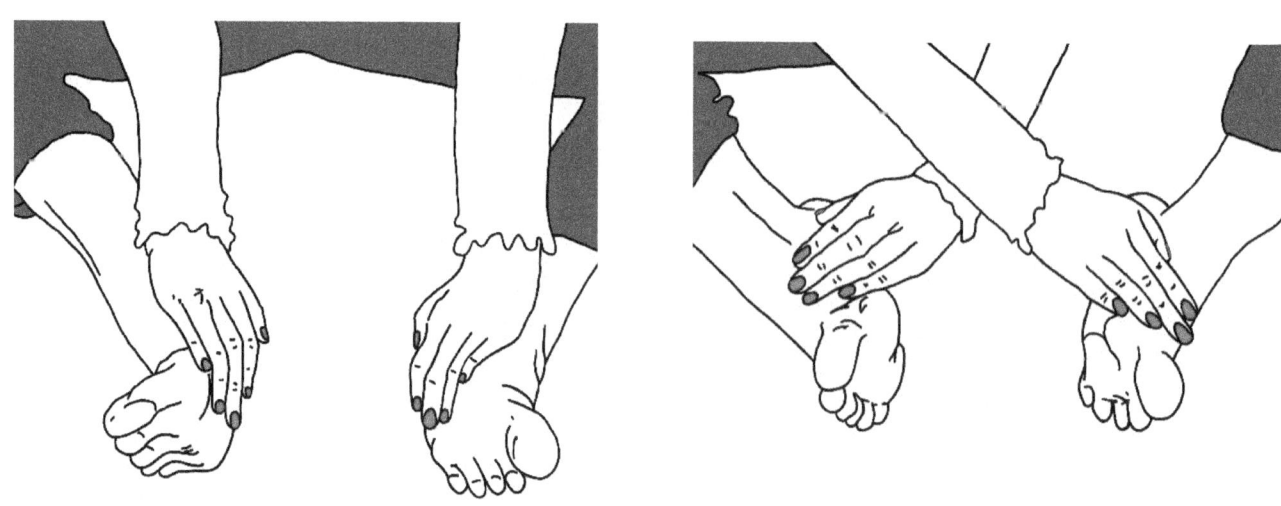

© 2024, Adrian Campbell, PhD

Alternative Sessions and Hand Placements

In addition to the methods discussed above, some Practitioners (including myself) experience greater sensation when they hover above the physical body approximately 2-4 inches. I highly suggest you try both, give a session touching and give one without, see which feels best to you.

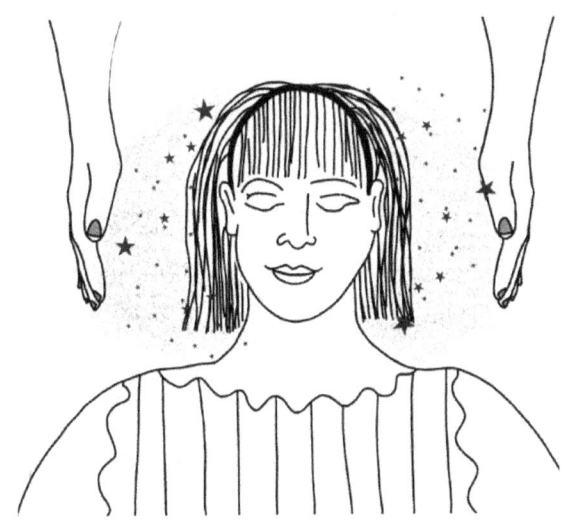

There may also be times that you can't physically reach the part of your body you would like to give Reiki to. If that happens you can simply beam Reiki at the intended body part, confident the Reiki energy understands your intentions and will respond in a way that serves your best interest.

Beaming Reiki also works well when you are sending Reiki energy to an object or being in the distance, working with animals, or when you are sending Reiki to a situation or something more general in nature.

Now Let's Practice… with a Guided Intuitive Self-Session Meditation

Below is a meditation to lead you into an intuitive self-session. This meditation will help you begin to tune in to your energetic body and identify any blocks that may be present.

Feel free to record yourself reciting this meditation and listen to it as many times as you'd like. At the end of the meditation, you are left to continue giving yourself Reiki as you are guided to do so. There is no specific time limit, you may take 5 minutes or 45 minutes, simply give yourself what you need, or what you have time for!

When I complete intuitive self-session of this style I often zone out, so to help bring me back to the real world, I often set a timer with a gentle tone.

Begin by finding a comfortable sitting position, one that will allow you to move your hands and arms freely. Once you have found your seat, I invite you to place your hands in prayer position. Ask that your ego be set aside, and if it is in your practice, feel free to take a moment and invite any guides you would like to help participate in this healing session.

The intention for this session is to heal whatever is in your best interest at this time. Take a moment and mentally state this intention to yourself, asking for whatever healing in in your best interest at this time.

Now, imagine your crown chakra opening up wide and ask for Reiki to flow. With your mind's eye, see the brilliant white light of Reiki energy flowing down into your crown chakra, down through the brow, the throat, into the heart and out of the hands. Concentrate for a few moments on the continuous flow of Reiki… into the crown chakra… and down into the heart and hands… into the crown chakra… and down into the heart and hands… into the crown chakra… and down into the heart and hands.

When you are ready, and only when you are ready, raise your hands, still pressed together, to just in front of your third eye. Ask for Reiki to guide your hands to where you need healing energy to flow. Remember to breathe, and be patient. Focusing on the flow of energy, down into the crown chakra… and down into the heart and hands… into the crown chakra… and down into the heart and hands…

As you feel guided to do so, move your hands to the place where Reiki wants to flow the most. Place your hands in this area and allow Reiki energy to flow from your hands to this part of your body. Remembering to keep your fingers together, and allowing yourself to either touch or hover just a few inches above the area, whatever feels best for you, but still focusing on the energy coming down into the crown chakra… and down into the heart and hands… and out into your energetic body… down into the crown chakra… and down into the heart and hands… and out into your energetic body…you may stay here for as long as you'd like, or as until you feel guided to flow Reiki in a different location.

Continue in this way until you feel you are finished or your timer goes off.

I encourage journaling after any Reiki self-session, as it helps anchor any healing energies here in the physical plane and can act as a reminder of things that may have come forward from beyond the conscious mind.

Remember that reflections can be anything you *feel*, and don't have to make sense to anyone, not even you. Written journal entries, images, or even just colors and shapes can all be helpful as we try to capture our experiences. Sometimes it is the simple lines that lead us to the greater discoveries down the road. It is up to you, use the space in your journal as you choose.

Chapter 4

Energy Healing for Specific Purposes

Using Reiki Symbols

So far you've been using Reiki without symbols, and as you move forward you may continue to do so, as they are not necessary to provide Reiki healing. However, the symbols that are given to you as part of your Level 2 Attunement are designed to focus your intention in specific ways, helping to guide the energy in a more direct fashion.

There are three symbols you will be empowered to use as a part of your Level 2 attunement; The Power Symbol, The Mental/Emotional Healing Symbol, and the Distance Reiki Symbol. Their true names are not mentioned in this book as a way to honor their sacredness. It is tradition that the symbols be kept confidential as a way to show respect for the power of the symbols, as well as to show consideration to others who have not been attuned and may try to use the symbols anyway, leading them to miss out on the true experience of Reiki.

Reiki symbols are transcendental, working not only with the conscious and unconscious mind, but also connecting directly to spiritual consciousness, communicating with the source of Reiki, Universal Consciousness. When you apply the symbols during a Reiki session the energy will change to match the intention you set.

The symbols can be thought of as buttons, that when "pushed" activate the energy of that symbol. They are activated through your intention to use them, which is supported through drawing the symbols. There is no perfect way to draw the symbols, but I highly encourage you to learn to draw them exactly as they are presented to you so that you can connect with the energy of all the others around the world and across time that have used them before you.

When you are shown the symbols and given an attunement by a Reiki Master, an imprinting takes place that links the image the student has been shown to the metaphysical energies the symbol represents. This creates an unconscious connection deep within you that will support your conscious intentions. By memorizing the image of the symbol, you reinforce this unconscious connection, allowing the energies of the symbol to be present whenever it is thought of.

To activate a Reiki symbol you may draw it in the air in front of you, in front of or over another being, or in the palms of your hands before starting a session. It is best to draw the symbols with your whole hand, being sure to leave the palm chakra open with your fingers closed but extended. You can also activate a symbol by thinking its name, by saying it out loud, or by visualizing it. As a new Practitioner I recommend you draw the symbol with your hand until you get to a point where the image is memorized. Once the symbol has been "drawn" you will want to "push" it in THREE times, one for each element of the human healer; mind, body, and soul. And that's it!

The Power Symbol

The Power Symbol comes from Shintoism, and can be understood to mean "by decree of the divine", and is used in a way similar to Christians saying Amen or Pagans saying So Be It. In Reiki practice the Power Symbol is used to increase the power of Reiki, or to focus Reiki energy in a specific area.

Using the Power Symbol can clear negative energies and seal the space around a living being, a place, or an object, protecting you, your loved ones, or your belongings from both physical and energetic threats.

To clear or seal energy, you can draw the symbol over your body, starting at the top of your head, at your crown chakra, and moving down to your base chakra. You can also draw the symbol over or in front an object or place.

I encourage you to use it at the beginning of your session by drawing the symbol on each of your seven major chakras and in the palms of your hands to increase the Reiki energy right from the beginning.

The Mental & Emotional Healing Symbol

The origin of the Mental/Emotional Symbol is Sanskrit and means love and harmony. This symbol is one that works to create balance in all things through love. It is helpful for mental and emotional healing, relationship problems, bad habits or addictions, nervousness, fear, depression, anger, sadness, and more. The Mental/Emotional Symbol can be used anywhere there is an energetic imbalance.

The Distance Healing Symbol

The Distance Healing Symbol is derived from a Japanese spiritual saying and is composed of kanji characters. The name of the symbol means "The origin of all is pure consciousness". Pure consciousness exists deep within us, connecting us to the energetic fabric of the world around us. When we can connect to this place there is no where in time or space that we cannot reach. With the Distance Healing Symbol you can send Reiki across the room, across town, across the world, and even across time.

I invite you to explore its full range by working with energies you identify as needing healing from past injuries, or even things that might have occurred in a past life, or in your ancestors' lives. Unfortunately, the Distance Healing Symbol can't erase past negative experiences, but it can ease any suffering or pain they may have caused.

You can also use the Distance Healing Symbol to create safety and protection in the future, by sending loving energy out ahead of where you will be going.

As a teacher I have used the Distance Healing Symbol to clear and seal my classrooms before I enter them, and I have sent distant Reiki to students and members of meetings I will attend, always with the intention that all who are present feel heard and loved. You can also send it out into the world, to different crises or situations that could use more loving energy. There really is no limit to how you can use this symbol, so I invite you to get creative with it.

There are many different methods to working with the Distance Healing Symbol, no one is better than the other, as it really comes down to personal preference. I have listed several below, try them out over time and decide which one works best for you.

- Using a teddy bear or other stuffed animal, etc. to take the place of a body... You can lay the placeholder on a table, in a chair, wherever you would normally be giving reiki if they were there in person. Prepare like you would for a normal session but also draw the Distance Healing Symbol over the placeholder (pushing it in three times) with the intention to connect to the person who should receive the Reiki. Then perform a session on the placeholder as if it truly was the person. When you are done, seal the session as normal.

- Using a picture … when sending distance Reiki to a person or place you can use a picture to help you focus your intentions. Simply draw the Distance Healing Symbol over the picture, "push" it in three times, and flow Reiki from your joined hands towards the photo. You can also place the photo between your palms and flow Reiki into it that way.

- Using a piece of paper… take a piece of paper and write the name of the person or situation you want to send Reiki to, then figuratively draw the Distance Healing Symbol over the piece of paper and "push" it in three times. Similar to the photo, you can beam Reiki at the piece of paper or place it between your palms.

- Using visualization... this method takes a bit more work, but I find the results to be worth it. You begin by visualizing a gate, draw the Power Symbol and Distance Healing Symbol on the gate, "pushing" each in three times. Next you open and walk through the gate, across a bridge, to a room with a door. When you open the door, you will see the place you are meant to give Reiki in. It may be a room with your intended recipient laying on a massage table or sitting in a chair, or it may be a location from your past that you want to send Reiki energy to, it is whatever you decide it should be.

    You stay in this room until you are finished giving Reiki, and then you walk out of the room, close the door behind you, walk back across the bridge, through the gate, closing it behind you, then drawing the Power Symbol on the gate, pushing it in three times and saying to yourself with each "push", "I seal this session with Love and Light". Then you may open your eyes and feel yourself once again back in the present. I also find it helpful to repeat the symbol name to myself during this practice as a way to maintain focus and connection to *where* I am doing the work.

    One note of safety with this method... please do not intentionally put yourself into a traumatic memory or event without the presence and support of a professional.

Remember that these are all suggestions. Reiki is a very individual experience and it is imperative that you follow your guidance with how to best work with the energy. Try a few of these out and feel free to combine or edit the methods into whatever works best for you.

Additional Uses for Reiki

Below is a list of additional ways to work with Reiki energy in your own life, but remember this is just the beginning, there really is no limit to what you can do with it! So feel free to get creative and explore different areas of your life where Reiki energy could be applied.

- Using the Power Symbol to clear & bless your home, workspace, etc. Anywhere you typically spend time really.

  To do this in a room, simply begin flowing Reiki, place your dominant Reiki Hand palm out toward one of the walls, draw the Power Symbol on the wall with Reiki, "seeing" with your mind's eye the white light flow from top to bottom, corner to corner as you push it in and say the name of the Power symbol, three times. Then repeat with the remaining three walls, floor and ceiling. Once you have drawn the Power Symbol on four walls, the floor, and the ceiling, place your hands out in front of you, palms down, and (just like closing a session) press down and say "I Seal this room with Love and Light" three times.

- Plants – Plants LOVE Reiki!!! You can Reiki the water you give them, or give Reiki directly to your plants, their soil etc. I often will charge a few quartz crystals as well and put them into my plants' soil – it's like a energetic "drip" system for them.

- Blessing food & water – Anything you give to yourself or others for nourishment can be sprinkled with loving Reiki energy.

- Aura Clearing – I like to do this in the evenings to clear my aura of the day's events and interactions. Simply flow Reiki and run you hands through the space around your body, through your aura, with the intention to clear away anything that does not belong to you or is not in your highest good.

- Reiki your bedroom and pillow for a good night's rest.
- Reiki your bath water before settling in for a relaxing bath.
- Reiki your shampoo, toothpaste, vitamins, medications… anything you use on or put into your body, Reiki just adds a little more healing energy and love.
- Reiki your computer, phone, or any other electronic gadget to help it stay "balanced" and in good working order.
- Use the Mental/Emotional Symbol to increase your focus and attention when working on a project or studying.
- Use the Distance Healing Symbol to send Reiki to anyone who is going into surgery – Reiki can help them tolerate the surgery better and can help them heal more quickly.
- Use the Distance Healing Symbol to send Reiki to any meeting in the future that you may be nervous about.
- Use Reiki to support creating healthier habits & empower your goals through intention and meditation, or by adding a healing pouch as described earlier. You can also create and charge a Reiki grid as described below in the same way.

Chapter 5

The Healing Power of Crystals

The Healing Power of Crystals

Crystals hold two types of power, innate power and assigned power. Their innate power stems from their geophysical properties and does not shift or change based on location, culture, or use. Their assigned power, however, is not necessarily static, and may change depending on who is using it and how.

For example, rose quartz has similar physical properties to clear quartz, which allows it to absorb and store energy, as well as any intentions associated with it.

Over the years, starting as far back as 7000 BC, rose quartz has been used as a form of jewelry or talisman. Romans used it as a seal of ownership, Egyptians believed it could prevent aging, and the early civilizations of the Americas believed it to be a "love stone", which is primarily what is us known for now.

As each of these civilizations attached their own specific meanings to rose quartz, they also energetically assigned the type of power it would emit. These power assignments are reinforced through cultural beliefs, and over time become a part of the energetic makeup of the stone.

This day and age, rose quartz is still commonly known as a "love stone", one that is related to the energies of the heart chakra, including compassion and self-love. If you meditate with rose quartz you can sense these energies, because they have been reinforced through belief and intention over thousands of years.

Now, all that being said… there are those who believe that stones come out of the earth with a set purpose ascribed to them by source, as well as inherent metaphysical properties that we can all use for our benefit.

Personally, as a Lumerian Crystal Healer, I believe that crystals, stones, and rocks (all the same thing really, just in different forms) are all an extension of Mother Earth and can be treated as a type of sentient being with needs and wants, just like a plant might have. I create a relationship with all the stones I work with, and to get the most out of your experience with them, I encourage you to do the same.

So, when you go to choose a stone for a specific purpose, try to keep an open mind. I invite you to visit a shop that you feel good about being in (vibe is important!), flow some Reiki into your hands and let your hands hover over the different stones. See which ones you are guided to work with, take a few minutes to hold them, resonate with them, *talk* with them. Don't limit yourself to stones that some book told you to use, just go out there and say Hi, see who says Hi back.

Using Reiki with Crystals

Clear quartz is THE stone to use in energy healing. As mentioned above its physical properties allow it told absorb and store energy, then slowly emitting it over a sustained period of time. Basically it was *made* for the work.

When you charge a quartz crystal it will absorb the Reiki energy from your palms, as well as any intention you send along with the energy. For example, If you wanted to charge a stone to help you focus more throughout the day, you would begin flowing Reiki as you would for any session, and then state your intention, as you would with any session, and then hold the stone between your palms and flow Reiki directly into the stone.

Some people find it helpful to create a mantra that supports your intention that you can repeat as you flow Reiki into your stone. For this example, something like this might work, "I am focused and calm, I am focused and calm, I am focused and calm".

I recommend doing this for as long as you'd like, but no less than 2-3 minutes. The longer you charge the stone, the more energy it will store. And YES, size does matter, haha! The bigger the stone the greater the capacity for energy storage.

Creating Crystal "Healing Bundles"

The simplest way to use stones in conjunction with your Reiki practice is to create what I like to call "healing bundles". Healing bundles are a nifty way to keep your intentions in one place, and when carried with you, they act as a physical reminder and energetic reinforcer, keeping you aligned consciously and unconsciously with your goals. I often make them for myself and my loved ones, as well as my clients. Once they are made up you can put them a pocket, purse, glove compartment, backpack, or even under a pillow.

To create a healing bundle, determine who the healing is for, what intention you would like to send, and then spend some time choosing which stones you think would best support this intention. Sometimes I have stones on hand I like to "re-use" and sometimes I need to do a little shopping.

If you decide to use a stone that has been in use for a different reason, maybe it's going from one healing bundle to another, be sure to clean and clear that stone. You can do this by burying it in the dirt (usually for a couple days), give it a bath (be sure it can handle water, Selenite for example will dissolve), or use Reiki. To use Reiki to clear a stone you simply flow Reiki into the stone with the intention to clean and clear the stone. You just want to be sure that whatever energy you put into it previously has been cleared before you charge it with something new.

After you decide who the bag is for, what your intention is, and what stones you want to use, you need to put it all together! I always have a few little velvet or mesh bags on hand, but you really can use any kind of bag you'd like.

In a typical healing bundle, I will have one quartz crystal, two additional stones that support my intention, and a small piece of paper with my mantra/intention/affirmation written on it. Below is an example of a bag I have made in the past for someone experiencing low self-esteem.

To charge the bundle, you will begin to flow Reiki as you would for any other session, then place the bundle between your hands and repeat your mantra while flowing Reiki into the bundle. Continue to do this for a minimum of 2-3 minutes, and then you can give the bundle to the person, place it on your altar, or carry it with you. If you have access to it, it is a good idea to re-charge it daily as a part of your morning practice.

Creating a Healing Bundle

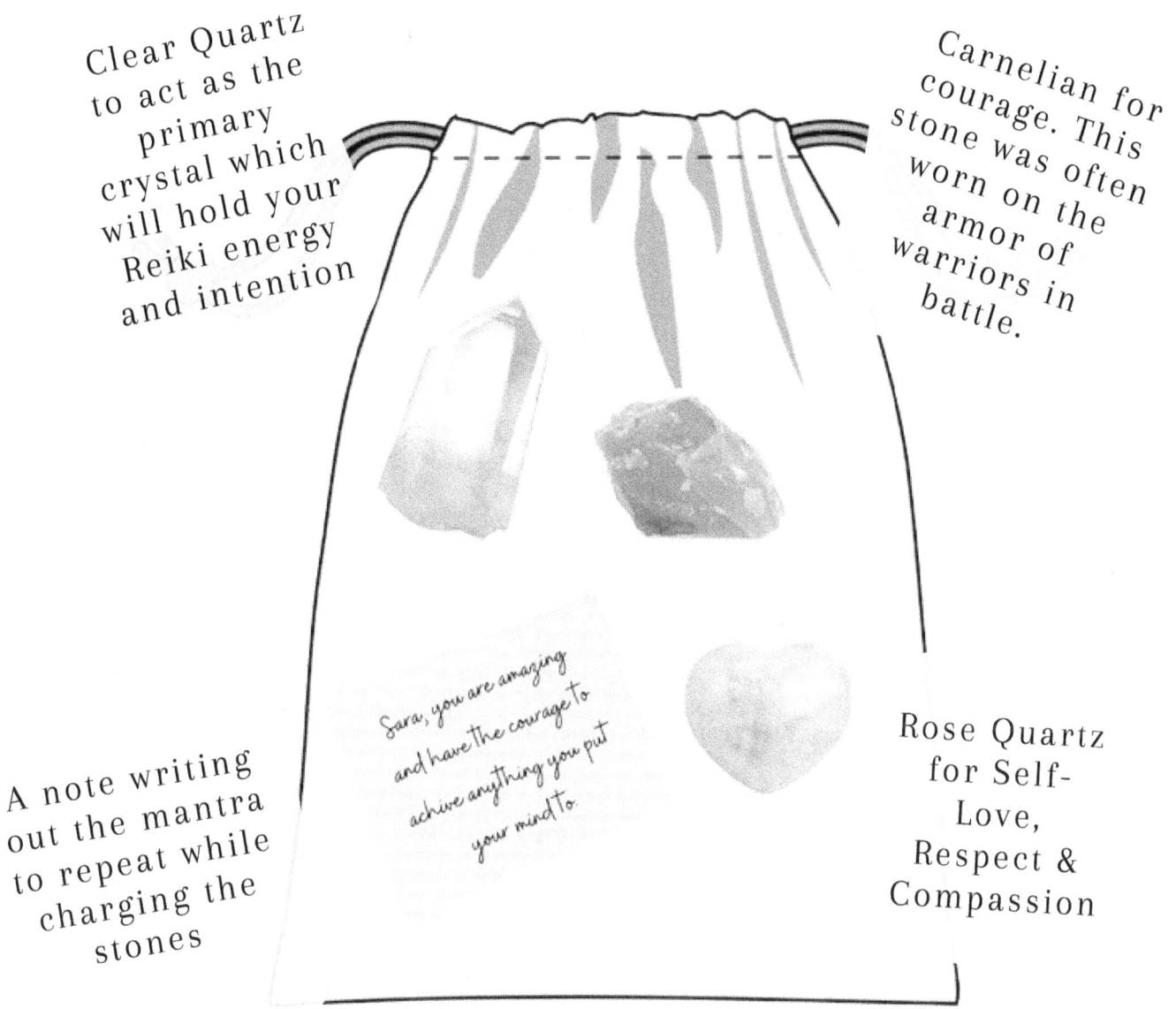

"In a crystal we have clear evidence of the existence of a formative life principle, and though we cannot understand the life of a crystal, it is nonetheless a living being."

~ Nikola Tesla ~

Creating Crystal Grids

Crystal grids are another great way to work with stones and energy healing. To create a simple crystal grid, you can start with 6, 9, or 12 quartz points and a center stone of your choosing. The size of the stones will determine how long the charge is held, but otherwise is unimportant.

The quartz points are the stones that will absorb, hold, and transmit the energy you infuse them with. The center stone should be a stone in alignment with your intentions. For example, in this image I have a light blue Angelite center stone, so this grid could be used to support throat chakra healing or to help me better connect with my higher self. The size of the center stone should align with the size of your quartz points.

Once the grid is charged it will continue to emit your intentions to the universe as long as it stays charged. How often you re-charge your grid will depend on the size of the stones and the length of your initial charging. I recommend checking in with it daily, perhaps as a part of your daily practice.

To Charge a Crystal Grid

1. Set up the stones on your grid like the one in the picture.

2. Take a moment to get your Reiki energy flowing and draw any symbols over the grid you would like, remembering to push each of them in three times.

3. Beginning at the center of the grid, use your whole hand, middle finger slightly lowered as a "pointer", to draw Reiki energy over the stones. Follow the pattern in the drawing beginning with #1.

4. As you trace Reiki energy over the stones, be sure to repeat you intention, as you are charging the stones with every pass.

5. Make a minimum of three rounds, and once complete, hold your hands over the grid (or draw a power symbol over the top of the grid), and repeat "I seal this grid with Love and Light" three times.

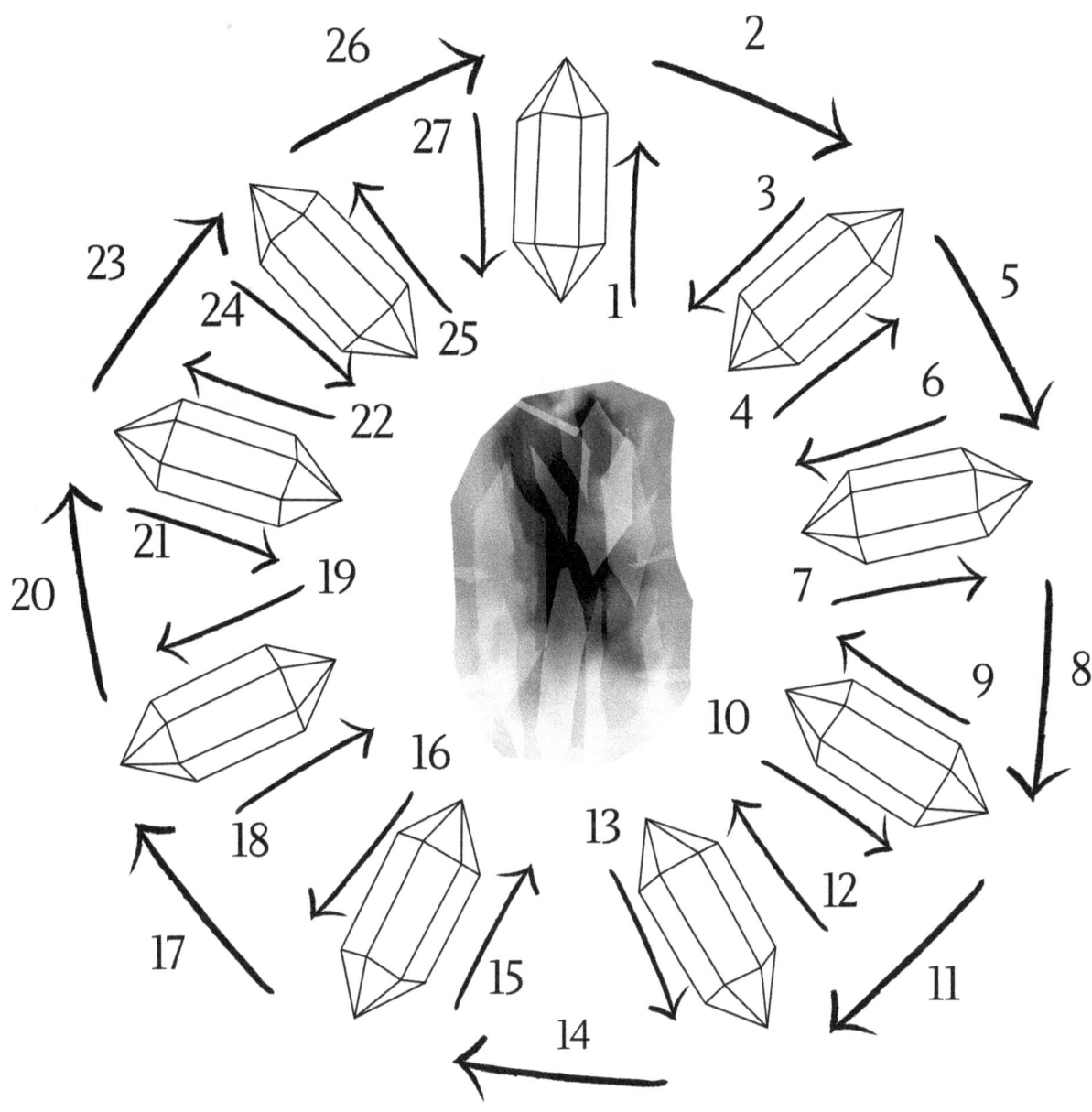

Chapter 6

Exploring Dis-ease through the Energetic Body

Exploring Dis-ease through the Energetic Body

As mentioned before, the energetic body encompasses our entire being, and the chakra system can help us view issues in the physical and mental/emotional body from a holistic perspective.

Each of the seven major chakras represents a specific type of energy and viewing our dis-ease through this lens allows us to explore these energies more individually, while they remain part of a whole.

1	Root/Base	Survival/Grounding/Prosperity
2	Sacral	Emotions/Sexuality/Family
3	Solar Plexus	Power/Autonomy/Will
4	Heart	Compassion/Self Love
5	Throat	Self-Expression/Communication
6	Brow/Third Eye	Intuition/ Creativity
7	Crown	Consciousness/Spirit

The seven major chakras connect to each other and are to be viewed and worked with as a system, however, they are often treated, and worked with, as discrete components which can limit healing opportunities. It is important to remember that the chakras work together to maintain balance throughout your energetic system. When one chakra is out of balance, the entire system is affected.

© 2024, Adrian Campbell, PhD

The lower half of the system (chakras 1-3) focus on the physical realties of our existence, and the upper half of the system (chakras 5-7) focus on more ethereal and imaginative states. Chakra 4 connects the upper and lower halves of the system, putting love and compassion at the center of all things. It is important that neither the upper nor lower half of the system is given preference, but rather, one should strive to bring the entire system into balance.

As mentioned previously, the chakra system is the metaphorical bridge between consciousness and matter, it is a part of our energetic body. The chakra system affects and is affected by our physical and mental/emotional body, displaying symptoms of disease through all three.

As we go through life, different challenging or traumatic life experiences map onto our energetic body. Examples of these types of experiences include, but are not limited to:

- Physical trauma, like broken bones, surgeries, or scarring.
- Mental and emotional trauma or abuse from family members, friends, and even ourselves.
- Generational trauma, which can be passed down just like any other genetic material.
- Past or parallel lives. Depending on your beliefs, the traumas we suffer in these other lives can be energetically carried across time and space.
- Empathic trauma absorption from others in your environment.

When these things occur consistently, or harshly enough, we can develop coping mechanisms that work to reinforce the dysfunctional energies, creating patterns that change the energy flow through the affected chakras, by creating dysfunction in the form of excessive or deficient energy flow, limiting our ability to experience life fully.

Types of Imbalances in the Chakra System

There are three primary ways imbalance, also known as chakra dysfunction, shows up in a chakra: excessive energy, deficient energy, and blocked energy. Most often when people talk about imbalances, they will say something like "your chakra is blocked". Though this may be true, it may be an assumption made by someone without enough knowledge to adequately assess the present dysfunction. It is more typical that a chakra will have excessive or deficient energy, than be blocked entirely.

An excessive chakra is an attempt to overcompensate for loss or damage by focusing excessively on that issue. For example, a bully is often someone who is insecure, and feeling a loss of personal power. To compensate for this loss, their Solar Plexus chakra becomes excessive, pulling the majority of their energy through that chakra, leading to behaviors which are overtly masculine, aggressive, and often oppressive.

Deficient chakras often stem from underdevelopment in a specific area, which can lead to avoidance due to lack of experience or fear. For example, someone who was often neglected as a child and lacks experience being in healthy attentive relationships, may have symptoms of an underactive heart chakra. Either that part of their system did not adequately develop, or they unconsciously restrict the flow of energy out of fear. This can cause an energetic deficiency which may display as an inability to create or maintain loving relationships with themselves or others.

When we consider a chakra blocked, it isn't that there is no flow at all, but rather that it is stuck in one direction or another. Imagine for a moment that each chakra has a valve that regulates how much energy flows in and out. If that chakra was blocked the vale would be stuck full open, or full closed. The flow could be either excessive or deficient, but the characteristic that makes it a blocked chakra is the inability to shift the energy.

Healing Dis-ease through the Chakra System

As the chakra system maps onto both body and mind, access to it can be found by a wide variety of methods. By understanding the connections between the chakra system and dis-ease in our lives, we can create a uniquely specific treatment plan that empowers us as individuals to heal ourselves.

To heal chakra dysfunction, you must address the problem on multiple levels:

1. Create understanding by learning about the dynamics of that particular chakra.
2. Create awareness through exploring the personal history related to that chakra's issues.
3. Take action by using different exercises and techniques to balance excess and deficiency.

Remember, that one method may not work for your entire system, and what worked one day, may need to shift the next, so it's important that you take a multidimensional approach. We are fluid beings and our approach to healing must be fluid as well.

Ways to work multidimensionally with chakra dysfunction:

- Verbally through Discussion – with friends, loved ones, a coach, therapist, or other wellness partner.
- Physically through work with the body and movement – yoga, somatic work, exercise, dancing, intentional attention.
- Spiritually through meditation – guided meditation, breathing, visualization.

- Emotionally through exploration of feelings – journaling, drawing, emotional release.
- Visually through images – daydreaming, visualization, dream boards.
- Aurally through sounds – mantra, chanting, singing, soul speak.
- Actualized through outer-world tasks that strengthen certain areas of our lives – skill building, intentional relationships, shift eating habits.

Understanding Energetic Contributions

Energetic contributions are made by the different experiences, injuries, situations, environments, relationships, beliefs or behavioral patterns, etc. that are now, or have once been, a part of your life, and they contribute to the overall state of your energetic body. They may stem from your own personal experiences, experiences from your past lives or those of your ancestors, inter-generational trauma, current situations or environments, habits you consciously or unconsciously have, or beliefs you hold to be true about yourself or the world at large. The benefit to addressing them through the energetic body is that energy flows through all three bodies, allowing the healing work you do to extend across your whole self.

Examples of past contributions can include birth trauma, difficulties with healthy attachment as a child, any abuse or neglect you have experienced throughout your life, traumatic accidents such as a car crash or natural disaster, grief over the loss of a loved one, severe financial difficulty, inherited shame or cultural trauma, rejection, betrayal, gaslighting, broken bones, surgeries, auto-immune disorders, and more. Though these things happened in the past, they may have lingering effects within not only your energetic body, but also your physical and mental/emotional body.

Examples of present contributions include any environmental, relational, or mental/physical/emotional issues you are currently dealing with. This includes your work environment, home environment, as well as the relationships you have with others and yourself. Too often we want to blame others for the state we are in, however, I implore you to go into this as open and honest with yourself as you can be. Our relationship with ourselves, including the way we treat ourselves, often has the biggest impact on our current situation in life. Current beliefs or mindsets, no matter where they came from, may be holding you in a certain energetic pattern. For example, making statements like "I can't do...", "I will never learn how to...", "I'm not smart enough for…", etc., are simple ways we unintentionally limit ourselves. I encourage you to be curious, brave, and full of grace as you explore the different areas of your current situation. Try not to blame yourself or others, but instead, try to focus on finding a solution.

A great way to key into current negative contributions is to explore any current symptoms of dis-ease you might have, both in the physical and mental/emotional body. For example, maybe you have noticed you always have digestion issues when you travel, symptoms of anxiety whenever you have to interact with certain people or be in a certain place, pain in your neck or shoulders, or maybe you get depression or insomnia at certain times of the year; all of these are symptoms of dis-ease and deserve to be looked into, even if you've been dealing with them for a very long time. Again, remember to give these things patience and grace, and try to move into it with curiosity over judgement. Sometimes it's the judgement or the demand to feel better right now that actually reinforces the block.

A Note on Exploring Your Energetic System…

This following section is designed to be informative, but also transformative. I invite you to fully engage with the material, understanding that you get out of this what you are willing to give.

As you progress through this section of the book, I encourage you to take the time to feel into each chakra as you read about it. Listen to what it has to share with you, think back to when you may have encountered any of the related traumas associated with the specific chakra, circle or make a note of any of the symptoms or traits that you may recognize within yourself. Take your time, and don't rush.

You will also be invited to makes notes about your past (energetic contributions) and present (contributors & symptoms) for each chakra. Again, take your time, allow what you feel to be present, not just your immediate conscious thought. You may even find it helpful to flow some loving energy into the specific chakra at the beginning of the section to create a higher level of resonance as you work with it.

Remember that what you see is merely a snapshot of what your system looks like today. A week, a month, a year from now things will look very different. I encourage you to approach this section, this moment of introspection, with kindness and grace.

Chapter 7

Exploring Your Chakra System

Base Chakra

Begin by placing a hand over the base chakra, flowing reiki into the chakra, creating an energetic resonance for you to tune into. Now as your read through the following information, circle anything that resonates with you.

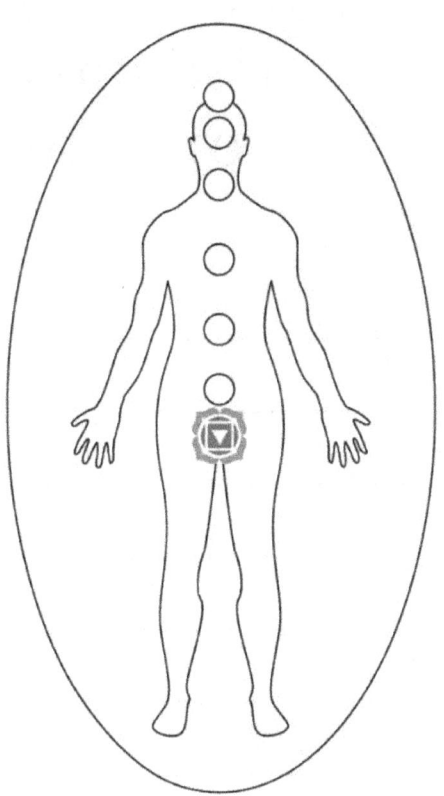

Name: Root, Base, #1

Purpose: Foundation, grounding

Element: Earth

Color: Red

Location: Base of Spine

Basic Right: To be here and have

Balanced Attributes: Good health, comfortable in body, sense of trust, ability to relax, well grounded, prosperity, stability

Traumas & Abuses: Birth trauma, abandonment, malnourishment, major illness or surgery, physical abuse, violent environment, inherited traumas

Deficient Attributes: Disconnected from body, underweight, poor focus, financial difficulty, poor boundaries, fearful, anxious, restless

Excessive Attributes: Obesity, overeating, hoarding, greed, material fixation, lazy, sluggish, fear of change, addicted to security, rigid boundaries

Physical Symptoms: Disorders of bowel, anus, large intestine, issues with legs, feet, knees, base of spine, buttocks, eating disorders, frequent illness

Take a few moments to reflect on the past & present energetic contributions to this chakra.

_____
_____
_____
_____
_____
_____
_____
_____
_____
_____
_____
_____
_____
_____
_____
_____
_____
_____
_____
_____

Base Chakra Healing Practices

1. Reconnect with body: As humankind has moved away from a natural life and into one of "reason" and industrialization, we have moved further and further away from our bodies.

To begin to reconnect, all you have to do is start paying attention. Notice the way you feel throughout the day… when does your body feel comfortable and relaxed? Uncomfortable or tense? What signs and signals is the body sharing with you that you have learned to ignore?

Pay attention and spend some time reflecting on what you notice. A body scan meditation has been included in the back of this book. Please feel free to record it and listen to it as many times as you'd like.

2. Physical activity, such as exercise, dancing, or yoga can all be helpful in healing the base chakra. Those activities which specifically include use of legs or being in touch with the earth can be especially helpful.

3. Touch can also be an effective way to provide healing energy to the base chakra. Whether it is a professional massage, cuddling with our pets, or hugging those we care for, the physical connection we experience can provide a sense of safety and grounding, which is the foundation of the base chakra.

4. Reclaim your right to be here. Throughout your life you may have had experiences which made you question whether or not you have a right to be here, to even exist at all. Well, let me tell you, you DO belong here. You are here as an essential and important part of this world, which could not exist as it is without you. Know this in your gut, feel it down to your toes, allow your roots to feel firmly planted in the earth, and tell yourself "I belong".

What are some of the ways you would like to support this chakra moving forward?

How could you add energy healing?

_____
_____
_____
_____
_____
_____
_____
_____
_____
_____
_____
_____
_____
_____
_____
_____

Sacral Chakra

Begin by placing a hand over the sacral chakra, flowing reiki into the chakra, creating an energetic resonance for you to tune into. Now as your read through the following information, circle anything that resonates with you.

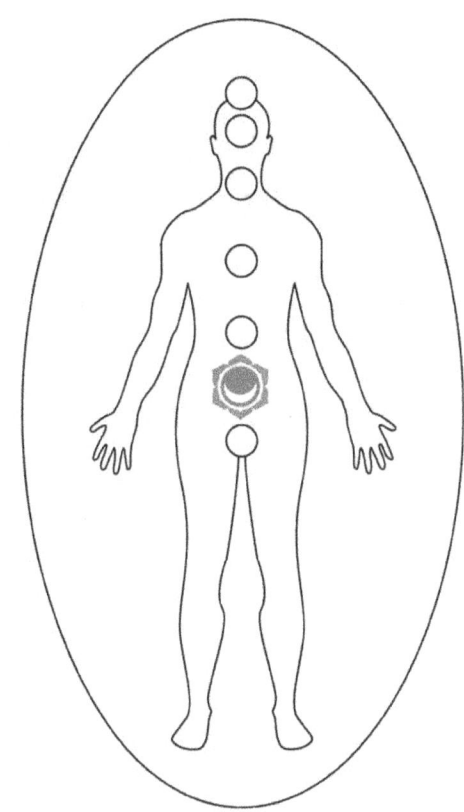

Name: Sacral, #2

Purpose: Movement, connection

Element: Water

Color: Orange

Location: Just below the navel

Basic Right: To feel and have pleasure

Balanced Attributes: Graceful movement, emotional intelligence, ability to experience pleasure, nurturing of self and others, ability to change, healthy boundaries

Traumas & Abuses: Sexual abuse, emotional abuse, volatile situations, neglect, rejection, denial of feelings as a child, emotional manipulation, moral severity, alcoholic families, inherited issues around sexuality

Deficient Attributes: Rigidity in body, frigidity, poor social skills, denial of pleasure, excessive boundaries, fear of change, lack of desire, passion, or excitement

Excessive Attributes: Sexual acting out/addiction, Pleasure addiction, excessively strong emotions, oversensitive, poor boundaries, seductive manipulation, emotional dependency, obsessive attachment

Physical Symptoms: Disorders of reproductive organs, spleen, urinary system, menstrual difficulties, sexual dysfunction, low back pain, knee trouble, lack of flexibility, deadened senses, loss of appetite for food, sex, life

Take a few moments to reflect on the past & present energetic contributions to this chakra.

_____
_____
_____
_____
_____
_____
_____
_____
_____
_____
_____
_____
_____
_____
_____
_____
_____
_____

Sacral Chakra Healing Practices

1. Movement Therapy: This can be as formal or informal as you'd like. You can work with a somatic therapist or practitioner, many can be found online through the International Somatic Movement Education and Therapy Association (ISMETA) at ISMETA.org.

Or, on the more informal side of things, you can attend a dance class designed to help encourage self-exploration and honor sensuality. A few examples include NIA, which is a fusion of dance, martial arts, and mindfulness, Authentic Movement which is an expressive improvisational movement practice that allows a group of participants a type of free association of the body, or even a Pole Dancing or Belly Dancing class.

2. Emotional release or containment as appropriate, inner child work, boundary work: Again, this can be done formally in a therapeutic setting, or on your own through methods you find helpful. The key is to acknowledge when it is time to seek out professional help. There is nothing wrong in using your resources and there are plenty of amazing therapists out here that have been training for years to help someone just like you.

3. 12-step program for addictions: The most well known 12-step program is AA – Alcoholics Anonymous, but did you know there are similar programs for narcotics, sexual addiction, gambling addiction and more? You can find a comprehensive list by doing a simple internet search for "12-step recovery programs".

4. Make time for healthy pleasures: Life for most of us is hectic and complicated. Mainstream culture dictates that we be productive and stay busy to be seen as an important and effective member of society. Unfortunately, that often means we put our own wants and needs aside. It is too common that in our efforts to please others we set aside the things that we find pleasurable in life.

What are some of the ways you would like to support this chakra moving forward?

How could you add energy healing?

___
___
___
___
___
___
___
___
___
___
___
___
___
___
___
___
___

Solar Plexus Chakra

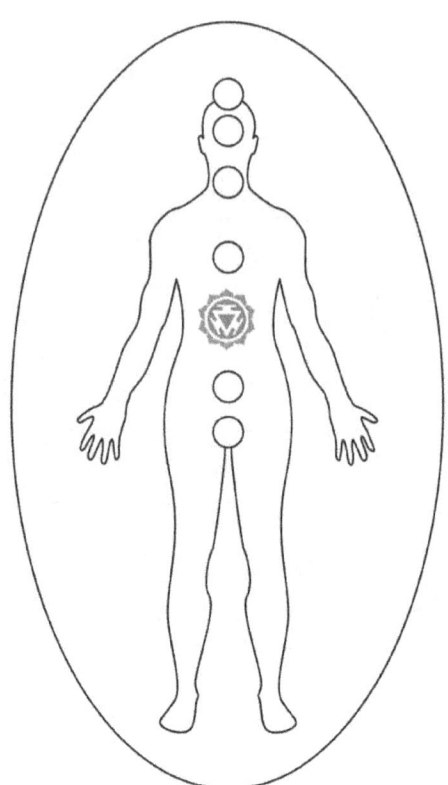

Begin by placing a hand over the solar plexus chakra, flowing reiki into the chakra, creating an energetic resonance for you to tune into. Now as your read through the following information, circle anything that resonates with you.

Name: Solar Plexus, #3

Purpose: Transformation

Element: Fire

Color: Yellow

Location: Solar Plexus (base of the breast bone)

Basic Right: To act and be an individual

Balanced Attributes: Responsible, reliable, good self-esteem, balanced ego-strength, warm personality, confidence, spontaneity, playful personality, appropriate self-discipline, able to meet challenges

Traumas & Abuses: Shaming, authoritarianism, volatile situations, physical abuse, dangerous environments, fear of punishment, inappropriate responsibilities as a child, inherited shame from parents

Deficient Attributes: Low energy, weak will, easily manipulated, poor self-discipline and follow through, low self-esteem, cold emotionally and/or physically, poor digestion, attraction to stimulants, victim mentality, passive

Excessive Attributes: Overly aggressive, dominating, controlling, need to be right, to have the last word, power hungry, manipulative, deceitful, attracted to sedatives, violent outbursts, stubborn, "Type A" personality, competitive arrogant, hyperactive

Physical Symptoms: Eating disorders, digestive disorders, ulcers, hypoglycemia, diabetes, muscle spasms, chronic fatigue, hypertension, disorders of stomach, pancreas, gall bladder, liver

Take a few moments to reflect on the past & present energetic contributions to this chakra.

_____
_____
_____
_____
_____
_____
_____
_____
_____
_____
_____
_____
_____
_____
_____
_____
_____
_____

Solar Plexus Chakra Healing Practices

1. Risk taking for deficiency: Try something new and get out of your comfort zone! Start with baby steps towards something you are interested in, but maybe never had the guts to do. Want to go scuba diving, start with snorkeling. Want to publish a book, maybe start by joining a local writing group. Build your confidence up slowly over time and remember it's OK to fail. Think of it this way… Fail = First Attempt In Learning!

2. Grounding and emotional contact help with both excess and deficient energy by connecting the rest of our system to provide the support we need to feel safe and loved exactly as we are.

3. Deep relaxation and stress control for excess: A great meditation to help create balance is Yoga Nidra. Yoga Nidra is a systematic method of guided relaxation which takes you to the place between awake and asleep allowing you to connect with your unconscious mind, and consists of eight stages: Relaxation, Awareness of Breath, Intention, Rotation of Consciousness, Opposite Sensations, Inner Space Visualization, Rapid Image Visualization, Repeat of Intention, and Return.

It is said that 30 minutes of Yoga Nidra is the equivalent to 4 hours of rest. A Yoga Nidra script has been provided at the end of this book. Feel free to record it and listen to it as many times as you'd like.

4. Vigorous exercise and martial arts can be especially helpful in releasing extra energy and expressing your strength of will. Running, biking, dancing, and are all great options. Choose something that resonates with you.

5. Psychotherapy, specifically for building ego strength, to work on releasing or controlling anger, issues with shame, and to encourage autonomy and strengthen willpower.

What are some of the ways you would like to support this chakra moving forward?

How could you add energy healing?

_____
_____
_____
_____
_____
_____
_____
_____
_____
_____
_____
_____
_____
_____
_____
_____

Heart Chakra

Begin by placing a hand over the heart chakra, flowing reiki into the chakra, creating an energetic resonance for you to tune into. Now as your read through the following information, circle anything that resonates with you.

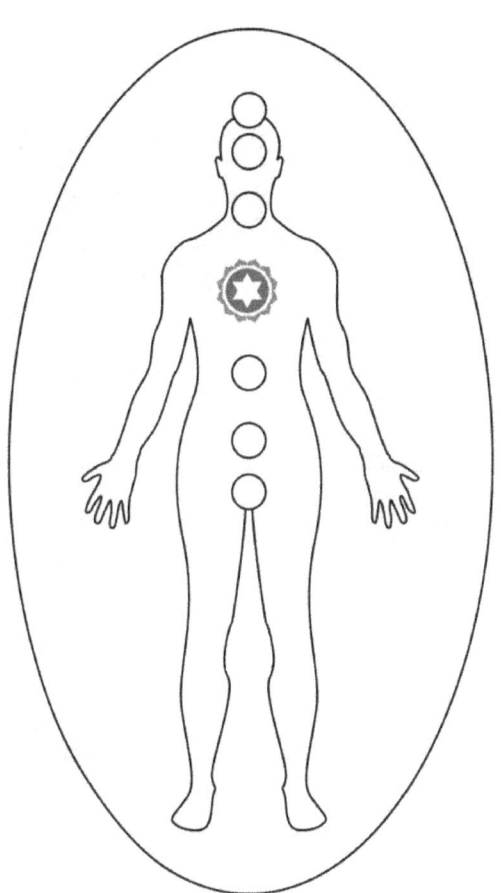

Name: Heart, #4

Purpose: Love, balance

Element: Air

Color: Green

Location: Center of the chest

Basic Right: To love and be loved

Balanced Attributes: Compassionate, loving, empathetic, self-loving, altruistic, peaceful, balanced, good immune system

Traumas & Abuses: Rejection, abandonment, loss, shaming, constant criticism, abuses to any other chakras, unacknowledged grief (including parent's grief), divorce, loveless/cold environment, conditional love, betrayal

Deficient Attributes: Anti-social, withdrawn, critical, judgmental, intolerant of self or others, loneliness, isolation, depression, fear of intimacy, fear of relationships, lack of empathy, narcissism

Excessive Attributes: Codependency, poor boundaries, demanding, clinging, jealousy, overly sacrificing

Physical Symptoms: Disorders of the heart, lungs, thymus, breasts, and arms, shortness of breath, circulation problems, asthma, immune system deficiency, tension between shoulder blades, pain in the chest

Take a few moments to reflect on the past & present energetic contributions to this chakra.

Heart Chakra Healing Practices

1. Breathing exercises: There are numerous types of breathing practices out there, many directed at specific outcomes like stress relief, anxiety reduction, or even lowering your body temperature. You can do them on your own or seek out a breathwork professional, either way the benefits can be immense.

2. Metta or Loving Kindness Meditation: This meditation uses words, images, and feelings to evoke a lovingkindness and friendliness toward oneself and others. It is recommended that you start with yourself, because the more love you have for yourself, the easier it is to share love with others.

Breathe gently and recite the following phrases directed to your own well-being.

May I be filled with loving kindness.
May I be safe from inner and outer dangers.
May I be well in body and mind.
May I be at ease and happy.

Repeat these phrases for five, ten, or even twenty minutes a day. When you feel ready to move on to others reference the full meditation at the back of this book.

3. Journaling, self-discovery: In every workshop I teach I talk about the importance of journaling. It helps get what *up there* down to earth so we can make it actionable, it helps us connect with the unconscious so that it may be more of a resource in our journey, and sometimes it just helps us get things out!

Too many times I have heard someone say "But I'm bad at journaling". No you're not. There is no right way to journal. Sure those bullet journals and fancy graphs and diagrams can be enticing, but none of that is necessary to help you process.

Often times when we work with dream images, emotions, or even experiences, words can fail us. We may stare at a blank page cursing ourselves for not knowing what to write, but let me tell you a secret, that is normal. These things are elusive by nature, and they don't necessarily want to be pinned down or defined. So how do we journal about them?

4. Psychotherapy, specifically to work on assumptions around relationships, emotional release of grief, forgiveness if appropriate, inner child work, codependency work, self-acceptance.

What are some of the ways you would like to support this chakra moving forward?

How could you add energy healing?

_____
_____
_____
_____
_____
_____
_____
_____
_____
_____
_____
_____
_____
_____
_____
_____
_____

Throat Chakra

Begin by placing a hand over the throat chakra, flowing reiki into the chakra, creating an energetic resonance for you to tune into. Now as your read through the following information, circle anything that resonates with you.

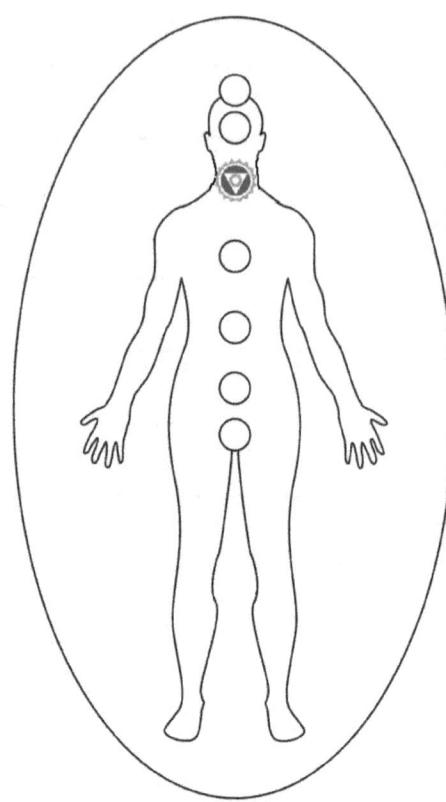

Name: Throat, #5

Purpose: Communication, creativity

Element: Sound

Color: Light blue, turquoise

Location: Throat

Basic Right: To speak and be heard

Balanced Attributes: Resonant voice, good listener, good sense of timing and rhythm, clear communication, lives creatively

Traumas & Abuses: Lies, mixed messages, verbal abuse, constant yelling, excessive criticism, secrets, authoritarian parents

Deficient Attributes: Fear of speaking, small/weak voice, difficulty putting feelings into words, introversion, shyness, tone deaf, poor rhythm

Excessive Attributes: Too much talking, talking as a defense, inability to listen, gossiping, dominating voice, interrupts

Physical Symptoms: Disorders of the throat, ears, voice, neck, tightness of the jaw

Take a few moments to reflect on the past & present energetic contributions to this chakra.

Throat Chakra Healing Practices

1. Loosen neck and shoulders: You may be surprised how tight we usually carry our neck and shoulders. Right now, take a minute and just notice them. Maybe roll your head from side to side, roll your shoulders forwards and backwards a few times… now how does that feel?

If this is something you'd like to work on, set an alarm on your cell phone for 3-5 times a day, reminding you to check in on your neck and shoulders. Journal on the experience each day and see what changes you notice after a week or two.

2. Singing, chanting, toning can be done on your own in the kitchen, shower, or while driving to work, with a professional voice coach, or even in a group choir. What you sing is only half as important as the intention, so feel free to let loose and have some fun if you'd like.

3. Storytelling is an extremely effective tool to help us find our voice and reconnect with our truth. There are therapists and coaches who specialize in this type of work, as well as support groups around the world that come together to write and share their stories with each other.

4. Journaling and automatic writing: Similar to journaling, automatic writing doesn't require good grammar or crafty sentences. Automatic writing is a way to just let things flow, not necessarily to be read or understood, but just to let what needs to come out, to get out. It can also help you connect to your unconscious mind and increase your creativity.

5. Practice silence for excess: Often when we have excess energy in our throat chakra we will talk and talk and talk and talk… keeping us from being able to listen and fully engage with the world around us. We can practice silence in multiple ways, some will be harder than others, so I invite you to start with listening and work your way up.

Listening can be done in a conversation by actively listening to what is being said without being worried about what to say in response, or by sitting silently in any environment and listening to the sounds around you, taking the time to notice each one and its unique contribution to the environment. Another option to try is a silent retreat, which can be done individually or with a group. This can be challenging for first timers, and some find that attending as part of a group provides an appreciated, yet unspoken support.

6. Psychotherapy specifically to learn communication skills and work on inner child communication.

What are some of the ways you would like to support this chakra moving forward?

How could you add energy healing?

_____
_____
_____
_____
_____
_____
_____
_____
_____
_____
_____
_____
_____
_____
_____
_____
_____

Brow Chakra

Begin by placing a hand over the brow chakra, flowing reiki into the chakra, creating an energetic resonance for you to tune into. Now as your read through the following information, circle anything that resonates with you.

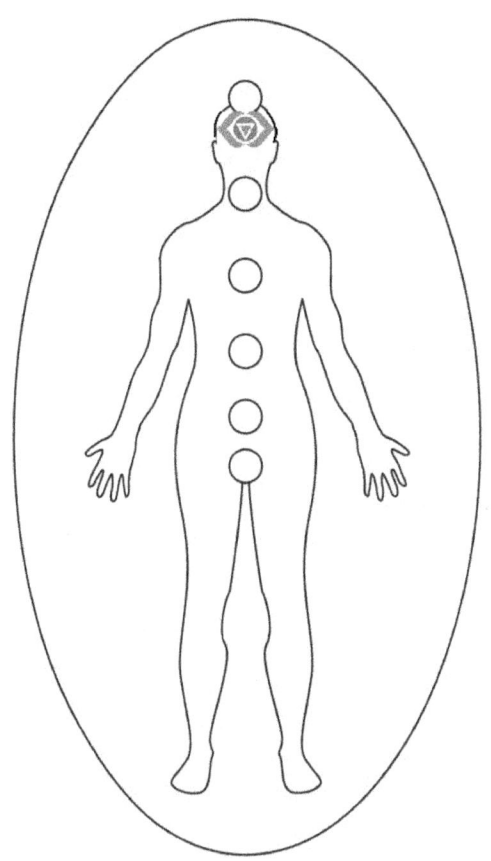

Name: Brow, Third Eye, #6

Purpose: Pattern recognition, Seeing beyond

Element: Light

Color: Indigo

Location: Forehead, brow

Basic Right: To be here and have

Balanced Attributes: Intuitive, perceptive, imaginative, good memory, good dream recall, able to think symbolically, able to visualize

Traumas & Abuses: Gaslighting (what you see doesn't match what you're told), invalidation of intuition and psychic occurrences, frightening environment (war, violence)

Deficient Attributes: Insensitivity, poor vision, poor memory, difficulty visualizing or seeing into the future, lack of imagination, dissociation from memories, denial, poor dream recall

Excessive Attributes: Hallucinations, delusions, obsessions, difficulty concentrating, nightmares

Physical Symptoms: Headaches and vision problems

Take a few moments to reflect on the past & present energetic contributions to this chakra.

_____
_____
_____
_____
_____
_____
_____
_____
_____
_____
_____
_____
_____
_____
_____
_____
_____
_____

Brow Chakra Healing Practices

1. Visual stimulation: through creating visual art like collages, mandalas, or something simple like your chakras. Art is about being able to express your imagination. Don't worry about being judged, just like with journaling, all you have to do is let it flow.

2. Meditation or guided visualizations: When the brow is deficient you will have trouble visualizing, and when it is excessive you wee *see* too much! Guided meditations help in both cases, by providing a foundation for the deficient to build on, and bumpers to help keep the excessive in the lane.

3. Psychotherapy, specifically art therapy, work with memory retrieval, connecting images with feelings, and past life regression

4. Dreamwork or hypnosis can also be very effective in healing the brow chakra as both work directly with the unconscious mind. Dreamwork can be done on your own or with a professional, whereas I would recommend you only attempt hypnosis with a professional.

What are some of the ways you would like to support this chakra moving forward?

How could you add energy healing?

_____
_____
_____
_____
_____
_____
_____
_____
_____
_____
_____
_____
_____
_____
_____
_____

Crown Chakra

Begin by placing a hand over the crown chakra, flowing reiki into the chakra, creating an energetic resonance for you to tune into. Now as your read through the following information, circle anything that resonates with you.

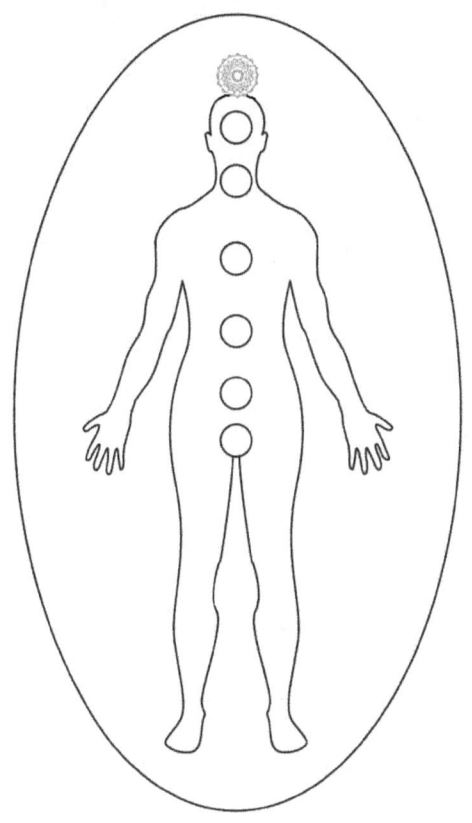

Name: Crown, #7

Purpose: Understanding, Connection to Spirit

Element: Thought

Color: Violet

Location: Top of the head

Basic Right: To know and learn

Balanced Attributes: Ability to perceive, analyze, and assimilate information, intelligent, thoughtful, aware, open-minded, spiritually connected, wise with broad understanding

Traumas & Abuses: Withheld information, forced religion, invalidation of one's beliefs, blind obedience, misinformation/lies, spiritual abuse

Deficient Attributes: Spiritual cynicism, learning difficulties, rigid belief systems, apathy, excess in lower chakras causing materialism, greed, domination of others

Excessive Attributes: Over intellectualizing, spiritual addiction, confusion, dissociation from body

Physical Symptoms: Coma, migraines, brain tumors, amnesia, cognitive delusions

Take a few moments to reflect on the past & present energetic contributions to this chakra.

Crown Chakra Healing Practices

1. Re-establish physical and emotional connection if in excess, by reconnecting with your lower chakras. Spend time grounding, being physically active, and with those you love to help calm excessive crown chakra energy.

2. Re-establish spiritual connection if deficient. This can be done through your choice of meditation or prayer. What matters most is what you believe to be true. We all have our own ways to connect, whether it be in a church, on a meditation cushion, or out in nature.

3. Learning and studying can help to re-energize a deficient crown chakra. The subject matter isn't necessarily important, what matters most is that you can ignite the passion for learning.

4. Spiritual discipline can benefit an excessive crown chakra, helping us to hone in on what matters most and focus our energy in a loving way.

5. Psychotherapy specifically to examine belief systems, develop an inner witness, and work with a higher power.

What are some of the ways you would like to support this chakra moving forward?

How could you add energy healing?

_____
_____
_____
_____
_____
_____
_____
_____
_____
_____
_____
_____
_____
_____
_____
_____
_____

Chapter 8

Co-Creating Your Future through Daily Practice

"Everything you need, your courage, strength, compassion and love; everything you need is already within you"

~ Anonymous ~

Co-Creation and Manifestation

Too often when we try to manifest our dream life we become overzealous with goals and commitments which end up harming us, instead of helping. Now, I'm not saying goals are a bad idea, but what I want you to consider is how limited your world view is. Spirit, the Universe, God, Goddess, whatever name you'd like to put on our higher power, just knows more, it sees more, it has a wider view available. When we become overly focused on a specific way of being, of how things are supposed to go, we limit ourselves. The gifts that are intended for us can't be delivered if we aren't open to accepting them.

As you begin to work more intentionally with your energetic body, your intuition will become enhanced, your connection to the world around you will deepen, and the universe will begin to move things out of your way, widening your path. It is imperative that you relax the reigns and allow for some flexibility in what comes.

To stay open but still work towards manifesting the life of your dreams I want to offer you the option of asking for what is in your highest good. This may or may not include things you are already aware of, but it leaves room for the gifts that are coming.

You can still work towards eating healthier, feeling more compassion, making more time to be with loved ones, even getting a better job, but I want you to try focus most of your energy on the why, not the how. Leave the heavy lifting of "how" things will work out up to the Universe.

Creating a daily affirmation or prayer is one of the most powerful ways to manifest what you want in life through co-creation with the Universe. Choose words that have a positive focus and that are simple to remember. Make them part of your everyday moments through a sticky note on the bathroom mirror, maybe one in the car, and even one on your desk at work. Play around with different options and ideas and see what resonates most with you. There is no wrong or right way, only the way that helps you the most.

To create the life you want, you need to first get clear about what that is. To manifest you need to LIVE the energy of the life you desire. When we create nothing but goals, we put all our energy into what if and when. Focus on what living that life will feel like, what emotions will be present in your body, what sensations will you experience on a daily basis. Figure these things out and then do everything you can to experience them now… THIS will align your energy with the future you want. Because let's be honest, we don't want the big house, the fancy car, the perfect butt, the most wonderful partner… we want how these things make us feel.

Take a few moments to focus in on your future, the life you want to create, and the feelings you want to experience...

___
___
___
___
___
___
___
___
___
___
___
___
___
___
___
___
___
___

Creating a Daily Practice

The following pages include daily practice and reflection sheets to help guide you in creating a meaningful and supportive daily practice.

So don't worry about getting it all done right now, just work on one thing at a time and trust the process.

There are extras of each page, and feel free to make copies of them and go through these steps again and again in the future as things change.

The daily practice you create should be fluid and shift just as your energy does. Reassess every so often and adjust your practice as needed.

Remember to focus on creating the feeling you desire, not the specific people, achievements, or objects that you believe will create that feeling for you. When you choose your healing methods, focus on how the methods themselves will contribute to the feelings you want to experience. Remember nothing is separate, and everything contributes to the energy we live within.

My Daily Practice

Date:

Focus Areas:

Intentions:

Activities or Practices:

Resources Needed:

Reflections from My Daily Practice

Monday

Tuesday

Wednesday

Thursday

Friday

Saturday

Sunday

Reflections from My Daily Practice

_____
_____
_____
_____
_____
_____
_____
_____
_____
_____
_____
_____
_____
_____
_____
_____
_____
_____
_____
_____

My Daily Practice

Date:

Focus Areas:

Intentions:

Activities or Practices:

Resources Needed:

Reflections from My Daily Practice

Monday

Tuesday

Wednesday

Thursday

Friday

Saturday

Sunday

Reflections from My Daily Practice

My Daily Practice

Date:

Focus Areas:

Intentions:

Activities or Practices:

Resources Needed:

Reflections from My Daily Practice

Monday

Tuesday

Wednesday

Thursday

Friday

Saturday

Sunday

Reflections from My Daily Practice

_____
_____
_____
_____
_____
_____
_____
_____
_____
_____
_____
_____
_____
_____
_____
_____
_____

Appendix

Meditations

Body Scan Meditation

Below is a simple Body Scan Meditation to help you begin to connect to your body through observation, acknowledgement, and gratitude. Feel free to record yourself reciting this meditation and then listen to it as many times as you'd like.

Begin by taking a few deep breaths to allow your mind to clear. Just breathe slowly and calmly, taking your time with each breath.

Breathe at your own pace...allowing each breath to come as it may, without any conscious effort to change your breathing.

This will be an exercise of observing. You will do a body scan and observe each part of your body passively...just noticing, without the need to make any changes or to cause anything to occur. You can simply watch and take note of any changes that happen on their own without any effort on your part. Let's begin the body scan.

Turn your attention to your toes. Focus on your toes, just noticing how your toes feel right now. Notice each toe.

Concentrate now on your right foot...just noticing your right foot without trying to change anything at all.

Now move your attention to your left foot...noticing how your left foot feels.

Observe both feet. How do your feet feel? Notice the temperature of your feet. Can you feel anything touching your feet? Clothing, the floor, the air? Notice how your feet feel inside. Heavy? Light? Loose? Tight? Make these passive observations...you are simply an observer...not providing any input at all.

Continue the body scan up to your ankles. Passively notice your ankles. Feel your ankles. Breathe.

Moving up now to your lower legs. Focus on your lower legs. Concentrate all of your attention simply on observing how your lower legs feel right now. Noticing. Observing. Completely passive...not trying to change anything.

Mentally scan your knees. Notice and observe each knee. Then take note of how your upper legs are feeling.

Notice your legs...taking note of any passive observations you become aware of. Just noticing...and then letting your attention move to the next area of the body.

Now notice your hips...

Your lower abdomen...

Moving up now all the way to the center of your body, at the level of your belly button...scanning your body...just noticing how the core of your body feels. Mentally watch and observe...taking in the details of how your body is feeling. Do a passive scan without making any changes or trying to make anything happen.

Notice now your middle back. Observe how your back feels.

Scan your sides...chest...and upper back. Noticing. Observing.

Turn your attention now to your fingertips. How do the tips of your fingers feel?

Continue...thoroughly scanning your body to observe how each area is feeling. Take note of your hands...notice the palms of your hands, and the backs of your hands. Breathe.

Scan your wrists...lower arms...elbows....

Turn your attention to your upper arms...noticing...observing...taking in your observations of how your upper arms are feeling.

Notice your shoulders. Scanning the front...sides...back...and top of your shoulders.

Scan your arms as a whole...noticing passively...allowing...watching...completely free of effort or direction from you.

Continue all the way up to your neck. Notice and observe your neck...the front of your neck...each side...the back of your neck.

Moving your attention up now to your chin...lips...cheeks...

Observe your nose...eyes...forehead...the top of your head...your ears....

Keeping this attitude of passive observation, mentally scan your body now as a whole. Do a complete scan, at your own pace, from your feet to your head.

If you notice anything of interest, you may choose to allow your attention to linger there for a moment as you observe how your muscles and tissues are feeling. Go ahead now and do a complete body scan, mentally observing your entire body.

You are fully aware now of how your body is feeling, and you have completed a body scan. Notice how you are feeling now, mentally and physically, overall. Observe any changes that may have occurred, all on their own.

Yoga Nidra

Yoga Nidra is a systematic method of guided relaxation which takes you to the place between awake and asleep allowing you to connect with your unconscious mind. This practice takes approximately 30-45 minutes to complete. A recording of this meditation is available on my website www.EnrgeticPsyche.com, or feel free to record yourself reciting this meditation and then listen to it as many times as you'd like.

You should begin by lying on your back with the knees slightly bent and supported… Make sure that you are warm enough and that your position is one that will be comfortable for the duration of the practice… It is best that you remain still during Yoga Nidra so that both your body and brain have a chance to fully relax, however if you become uncomfortable, please feel free to change position… Allow your eyes to close and keep them closed until the practice has ended.

The practice of Yoga Nidra is a practice of yogic sleep that will guide you to the hypnagogic state, a state of consciousness between wakefulness and sleeping. Try to remain awake by listening to the sound of my voice. You will be asked to move your awareness to various bodily sensations, emotions, and images. Try not to concentrate too intensely as this may prevent you from relaxing. During this meditation, please use and absorb what you need in the moment and leave the rest behind. If the mind becomes overactive with thoughts and worries, just come back to the sound of my voice.

Become aware of any sounds you can hear in this moment. Whatever you can hear without strain… Begin to focus on the most distant sounds that you can hear… Let your sense of hearing radiate outward, searching out these distant sounds and following them for a few moments…Move your attention from sound to sound without labeling the source… Gradually bring your attention to closer sounds… move your attention to the sounds outside this building… to sounds inside this building… to sounds inside the room…

Without opening your eyes visualize the four walls of this room, the ceiling, the floor, your physical form, resting on your mat… Visualize yourself lying on the floor, the position of your body, your clothes, your hair, your face. Become acutely aware of the existence of your physical form lying on the floor.

Become aware of your natural breath, become aware of your natural and spontaneous breath that moves in and out of your body without any effort... The natural breath flows in through both nostrils. Notice the feeling of the breath as it comes in and out of your nostrils… There is a sense of coolness as you inhale the breath… Follow this feeling into your nose, your sinuses, the back of your throat, into your lungs… There is a sense of warmth as you exhale the breath. Feel this warmth on your upper lip as you breathe out…

The natural breath flows through both nostrils during the inhale and the exhale… Allow your breath to become longer and slower…Take a long slow inhalation, followed by a longer slower exhalation. Make your exhale even slower - notice the slight pause after the exhale. Slow inhale, even slower exhale, and pause. Feel the urge to breathe in bubble up inside of you. When you need to inhale, please do so. Long slow inhale, longer slower exhale, and then pause where the body is neither breathing in nor out. Please continue breathing in this way for the next few moments… Now go back to the natural easy breath, releasing any control over the inhale or exhale.

At this moment you should make your intention. The intention should be a short, positive statement in simple language; try to discover one naturally, just relax and see what comes to mind… Please mentally state your intention to yourself clearly and with awareness three times. The intention you make during yoga nidra plants a seed deep in the fertile soil of your mind to bring about transformation and healing.

Also say to yourself, "I am practicing yoga nidra, I am awake and relaxed."

We will now begin a systematic journey of sensory awareness throughout the body. You will move your awareness to different parts of your body as soon as you hear them named. Please say the name of the part to yourself and feel that part of your body but do not move any part. The practice begins on the right side.

Right hand thumb … 2nd finger … 3rd finger … 4th finger … 5th finger … palm of the hand … back of the hand …wrist … forearm … elbow … upper arm … shoulder … armpit … waist … hip … thigh … knee … calf … ankle … heel …sole of the foot … top of the foot … right big toe … 2nd toe … 3rd toe … 4th toe … 5th toe. Left hand thumb … 2nd finger … 3rd finger … 4th finger … 5th finger … palm of the hand … back of the hand … wrist … forearm … elbow … upper arm … shoulder … armpit … waist … hip … thigh … knee … calf … ankle … heel … sole of the foot … top of the foot … left big toe … 2nd toe … 3rd toe … 4th toe … 5th toe. Now go to the back of the body … right heel … left heel … right calf … left calf … right thigh … left thigh … right buttock… left buttock … lower back … middle back … upper back … the entire spine … right shoulder blade … left shoulder blade … back of the neck … back of the head. Top of the head … forehead … right temple … left temple … right ear … left ear … right eyebrow … left eyebrow … middle of the eyebrows … right eye … left eye … right nostril … left nostril … right cheek … left cheek … upper lip … lower lip … both lips together … chin … jaw … throat … right collarbone … left collarbone … right side of the chest … left side of the chest … upper abdomen … navel … lower abdomen … right groin … left groin … the pelvic floor.

Your whole right leg … whole left leg … whole right arm … whole left arm … Your whole face … Your whole head … Your whole torso … Your whole body … Your whole body … Your whole body.

Now imagine your whole body becoming light. As though you could float away from the floor and toward the ceiling… The head is light and weightless, the limbs are light and weightless, the torso is light and weightless, your whole body light and weightless… You are rising higher and higher away from the floor… Imagine your body becoming heavy… Feel the heaviness in all parts of your body, each part is becoming heavier and heavier and heavier… The head is heavy, the limbs are heavy, the torso is heavy, your whole body is heavy. So heavy that the floor comes up to support you… now release the sensations of heaviness in the body.

Awaken the experience of cold in your body, the experience of chilly cold… Imagine being outside in winter without enough clothing… You feel this chill permeating your entire being... Now allow the sensation of warmth to spread throughout your entire body… Remember the feeling of heat in summer when you are out in the sun with no shade... You feel heat radiating onto your skin, heat all around …Then, sense both cold and heat simultaneously. …Sense how this acts on your entire body and mind… then release the sensations of cold and heat in the body.

Now welcome an emotion that's present in your body… or recall a specific emotion that you'd like to work with in this moment. … If it's helpful, recall a memory that invites this emotion more fully into your body. … And if no emotion is present, this, too, is your experience, everything just as it is. … Be with what's most calling your attention right now… whether an emotion, a feeling, or another sensation.

If an emotion is present, where in your body do you feel it? Are there thoughts or images that accompany this emotion?…Welcome your experience just as it is without judging it or trying to change it. …Now, locate an opposite emotion and where you experience this opposite in your body. …If it's helpful, recall a memory that invites this opposite of emotion more fully into your body. …Then, move back and forth between these opposites, experiencing first one, then the other, in your own rhythm. …Sense how each emotion affects your body and mind. …Then, sense both emotions simultaneously. …Sense how this acts on your entire body and mind. …release the sensations of the emotions and return your awareness to the natural breath.

Begin to concentrate on the space in front of your closed eyelids. Imagine that in front of you there is a screen as though you were at the movie theatre. The screen is as high and as wide as the eyes can see. Concentrate on this mind screen and become aware of any phenomena that manifests within it; colors, patterns and light. Whatever you see is the manifesting state of your mind. Continue your awareness of this space but do not become involved, practice detached awareness only. If any subtle images make themselves known, simply notice them without directing the images. If thoughts occur let them come and go but continue watching the dark space, continue this with detached awareness.

Now, a number of different things will be named and you should envision them on the level of emotion, memory, and imagination as best you can. Move from image to image as soon as you hear the new one named.

Peacock feather …

Buddha meditating …

A good night's rest ...

Full moon ...

Your reflection in a mirror ...

Foggy morning ...

Sun shining overhead ...

Bouquet of flowers ...

Tall tree …

Receiving help from others ...

Cool clear water ...

Making appointments …

A relaxing afternoon…

Laughing with friends…

A warm embrace…

Burning candle ...

Temple on a mountain ...

Path in the woods ...

Vibrant sunset ...

Taking a deep breath ...

Cat stretching ...

A beautiful garden path…

Your favorite song…

The sound of my voice…

It is time to repeat your intention. Please mentally repeat the same statement made at the beginning of the practice three times.

Come back to the feeling of your breath flowing in and out of your nostrils. Maintain your awareness of breath and at the same time develop your awareness of your physical body. Your body is relaxed and lying on the mat. Feel the container of your skin and the clothes that are touching you. Notice the heaviness of your body as it rests on the floor and take your awareness into all the points that are being supported by the floor; the back of your heels, thighs, buttocks, shoulder blades, arms, hands and head. Do not open your eyes yet, but visualize the surrounding room. Imagine where you are in the room and the other objects that are around you. Lie quietly until you feel ready to move. Start by slowly moving your hands and feet, take your time, there is no hurry. When you are sure that you are fully awake, gently open your eyes. Please roll over to your side. Stay on your side for a few more moments. Use your hands to gently press yourself up from the floor.

The practice of Yoga Nidra is now complete.

Lovingkindness – Metta Meditation

This meditation is taken with gratitude from the book, "The Art of Forgiveness, Lovingkindness, and Peace" by Jack Kornfield

This meditation uses words, images, and feelings to evoke a lovingkindness and friendliness toward oneself and others. With each recitation of the phrases, we are expressing an intention, planting the seeds of loving wishes over and over in our heart. With a loving heart as the background, all that we attempt, all that we encounter will open and flow easily.

You can begin the practice of lovingkindness by meditating for fifteen or twenty minutes in a quiet place. Let yourself sit in a comfortable fashion. Let your body rest and be relaxed. Let your heart be soft. Let go of any plans and preoccupations.

Begin with yourself. Breathe gently, and recite inwardly the following traditional phrases directed to your own well-being. You begin with yourself because without loving yourself it is almost impossible to love others.

>May I be filled with lovingkindness.
>
>May I be safe from inner and outer dangers.
>
>May I be well in body and mind.
>
>May I be at ease and happy.

As you repeat these phrases, picture yourself as you are now, and hold that image in a heart of lovingkindness. Or perhaps you will find it easier to picture yourself as a young and beloved child. Adjust the words and images in any way you wish. Create the exact phrases that best open your heart of kindness. Repeat these phrases over and over again, letting the feelings permeate your body and mind. Practice this meditation for a number of weeks, until the sense of lovingkindness for yourself grows.

Be aware that this meditation may at times feel mechanical or awkward. It can also bring up feelings contrary to lovingkindness, feelings of irritation and anger. If this happens, it is especially important to be patient and kind toward yourself, allowing whatever arises to be received in a spirit of friendliness and kind affection.

When you feel you have established some stronger sense of lovingkindness for yourself, you can then expand your meditation to include others. After focusing on yourself for five or ten minutes, choose a benefactor, someone in your life who has loved or truly cared for you. Picture this person and carefully recite the same phrases:

> May you be filled with lovingkindness.
>
> May you be safe from inner and outer dangers.
>
> May you be well in body and mind.
>
> May you be at ease and happy.

Let the image and feelings you have for your benefactor support the meditation. Whether the image or feelings are clear or not does not matter. In meditation they will be subject to change. Simply continue to plant the seeds of loving wishes, repeating the phrases gently no matter what arises.

Expressing gratitude to our benefactors is a natural form of love. In fact, some people find lovingkindness for themselves so hard, they begin their practice with a benefactor. This too is fine. The rule in lovingkindness practice is to follow the way that most easily opens your heart.

Blank page

www.ingramcontent.com/pod-product-compliance
Lightning Source LLC
Chambersburg PA
CBHW081232170426
43198CB00017B/2740